Cambridge Elements ☰

Elements in Publishing and Book Culture
edited by
Samantha Rayner
University College London
Leah Tether
University of Bristol

SPACE AS LANGUAGE

The Properties of Typographic Space

Will Hill
Anglia Ruskin University

CAMBRIDGE
UNIVERSITY PRESS

Shaftesbury Road, Cambridge CB2 8EA, United Kingdom

One Liberty Plaza, 20th Floor, New York, NY 10006, USA

477 Williamstown Road, Port Melbourne, VIC 3207, Australia

314–321, 3rd Floor, Plot 3, Splendor Forum, Jasola District Centre,
New Delhi – 110025, India

103 Penang Road, #05–06/07, Visioncrest Commercial, Singapore 238467

Cambridge University Press is part of Cambridge University Press & Assessment,
a department of the University of Cambridge.

We share the University's mission to contribute to society through the pursuit of
education, learning and research at the highest international levels of excellence.

www.cambridge.org
Information on this title: www.cambridge.org/9781009265430

DOI: 10.1017/9781009265447

© Will Hill 2023

This publication is in copyright. Subject to statutory exception and to the provisions
of relevant collective licensing agreements, no reproduction of any part may take
place without the written permission of Cambridge University Press & Assessment.

First published 2023

A catalogue record for this publication is available from the British Library.

ISBN 978-1-009-26543-0 Paperback
ISSN 2514-8524 (online)
ISSN 2514-8516 (print)

Cambridge University Press & Assessment has no responsibility for the persistence
or accuracy of URLs for external or third-party internet websites referred to in this
publication and does not guarantee that any content on such websites is, or will
remain, accurate or appropriate.

Space as Language

The Properties of Typographic Space

Elements in Publishing and Book Culture

DOI: 10.1017/9781009265447

First published online: August 2023

Will Hill

Anglia Ruskin University

Author for correspondence: Will Hill, will.hill@aru.ac.uk

ABSTRACT: This Element examines the function and significance of typographic space. It considers in turn the space within letters, the space between letters, the space between lines, and the margin space surrounding the text-block, to develop the hypothesis that viewed collectively these constitute a 'metalanguage' complementary to the text. Drawing upon critical perspectives from printing, typeface design, typography, avant-garde artistic practice and design history, the Element examines the connotative values and philosophies embodied in the form and disposition of space. These include the values attributed to symmetry and asymmetry, the role of 'active' space in the development of modernist typography, the debated relationship between type and writing, the divergent ideologies of the printing industry and the letter arts, and the impact of successive technologies upon both the organisation and the perception of typographic space.

KEYWORDS: typography, layout, printing, fonts, design

ISBNs: 9781009265430 (PB), 9781009265447 (OC)

ISSNs: 2514-8524 (online), 2514-8516 (print)

Contents

Introduction: Reading the Space

'We put thirty spokes together and call it a wheel;
But it is on the space where there is nothing
That the usefulness of the wheel depends.
We turn clay to make a vessel;
But it is on the space where there is nothing
That the usefulness of the vessel depends.
We pierce doors and windows to make a house;
And it is on these spaces where there is nothing
That the usefulness of the house depends.
Therefore just as we take advantage of what is,
We should recognize the usefulness of what is not.'
Lao Tzu *Tao Te Ching* Tr. Arthur Waley[1]

'The Japanese had a word (*ma*) for this interval which gives shape to the whole. In the West we have neither word or theme. A serious omission.' (Alan Fletcher[2])

The design of a book page draws upon a matrix of related bodies of expertise, including the design of typefaces, the setting of lines of type and the disposition of these lines within the space of the page. These are traditionally associated with the disciplines of typeface design, typesetting and book design, and are normally considered from within the critical and practical literature of these subjects. The common properties which link and relate these choices are properties of space, and it is the understanding of typographic space at each of these levels of the design that enables the designer to relate these aspects to each other, to achieve a harmonious whole. This book will explore the interrelated nature of these different orders of typographic space to construct an expanded view of the subject as a single totality and consider this totality as a coherent visual language,

[1] Li Er Lao Tzu, *Tao Te Ching*, Translated by A. Waley, and R. Wilkinson (Ware: Wordsworth, 1997)
[2] A. Fletcher, *The Art of Looking Sideways* (London: Phaidon, 2003)

providing a critical context for the development of wider perspectives upon both designing and reading.

In the activity of reading the printed page we engage with a complex of interrelated relationships of shape and space. These include the interior spaces that characterise each letter and distinguish it from its neighbour, the intervals that define and separate the shapes of words, the 'weave' of space between lines, and the margins that relate the limits of the text area to the material limits of the page. These variables combine to determine ease of use, but also to inform our wider 'reading' of the page, evoking connotative values and signalling philosophical preferences. The designer of our page will have drawn upon several related bodies of specialist knowledge. The professional literature of the subject identifies complex and detailed practical decisions, around which different design ideologies have evolved. Designers and typographers agree on the importance of negative space, from a variety of different viewpoints. Stanley Morison included in his definition of typography the process of 'distributing the space'[3] while Jan Tschichold stated that 'the white background plays an active part in the design'.[4]

Critical perspectives on typography continue to be informed by the material history of printing. Traditionally, typographic space has been the outcome of tangible material processes. For 500 years, printers and typographers organised the two-dimensional space of the page by physical means, through the relationships of three-dimensional components. The first of these was the typeface, originated as a three-dimensional 'punch': a sculpture of the letter in reverse, crafted by the removal of metal from the face of a steel rod; defined by the introduction of space into mass. The punch was then struck to create a right-reading matrix from which multiple reverse-reading impressions could be cast. The resulting metal letters or 'sorts' would be organised into lines of words by the compositor disposing the letters and spaces, by hand up to the late nineteenth century and subsequently through the machine composition systems of Linotype and Monotype. These lines of type would be arranged in the composing stick,

[3] S. Morison, *First Principles of Typography* (Lieden: Academic Press Leiden, 1996), p. 3.
[4] J. Tschichold, *The New Typography*, Translated by R. McLean (Oakland: University of California Press, 1998), p. 72

strips of lead would be inserted between them to determine line-spacing, and additional space added to fill out the column width and enable a rectangular print area to be locked within the frame of the chase. Space was therefore a tangible material in the compositor's hand, a codified system of material parts: metal spaces of various widths and strips of lead of standardised thickness, both related to the typographic letters by a common system of measurement in points. The unprinted areas of the page were therefore determined by the placing of space materials that had physical mass and weight, names and measurements. From the mid-twentieth century, as metal setting was replaced by photosetting and then by digital type, this material space became instead a 'virtual' concept, but the material traditions of metal type persist both in the user expectations of the reader and in much of the language of typography.

Technological change prompted some revised perspectives upon the nature of typographic space. In the 1968 edition of his 1960 *The Visible Word*, Herbert Spencer notes that 'much research this century has been concerned with questions of line length, interlinear spacing, margins and other aspects of the use of space in typography' and continues, 'Spatial arrangements . . . which have been established as optimum for the printed page held in the hand need now to be reconsidered in relation to images projected onto a television screen or microfilm viewer'.[5] Since that time, digital media for both typesetting and typeface design have developed in sophistication to encompass the refinements of previous technologies while adding further capabilities, many of them prompted by the new challenges of the transition from the printed page to the screen. The semantic properties of typographic space apply equally in both contexts, determining the way that the spatial typography of the page reflects and advances the conceptual structure of the text. The web designer Mark Boulton has noted the fundamental idea that graphic structures can reflect conceptual structures, 'Making sure the graphical representation of the content matches the mental model of the reader',[6] while David Crystal has identified the

---

[5] H. Spencer, *The Visible Word* (London: Royal College of Art, 1968), pp. 11–12

[6] M. Boulton, *Semantic Typography: Bridging the XHTML Gap* (2005). Retrieved 24 October 2022, from https://markboulton.co.uk/journal/semantic-typography-bridging-the-xhtml-gap/

need 'for linguists to become more interested in the properties of graphic substance'.[7] The disposition of typographic space is foremost among these properties. Johanna Drucker affirms that white space 'is not inert, not pregiven and neutral, not an a priori fact or entity, but is itself relational and constituted through dynamic relations.'[8] Both the microtypography of typographic detailing (font, case, spaces, dashes, indents) and the macro-typography of the page space (margins, columns, grids) invite multiple levels of interpretation. The disposition of space can signal design ideologies and cultural connotations. A generous volume of white space signifies added value, whether in luxury goods or linguistic messages. Across western visual culture, placing an object within a larger space (or adding a designed space around it) 'frames' that object to invite enquiry and interpretation. The white space of the page is a vessel containing the textual meaning, and the arrangement of type within that space directs the conditions of reading and the expectations that the reader brings to the text. Space is therefore both the connective tissue of printed language, and its paratextual frame. Typographic space as a 'structural agent' was a key precept of the concrete poetry movement of the 1950s.[9] One defining characteristic of poetry is the idea of an ordered relationship between its parts; typically by patterns of metre and rhyme. This may involve symmetries and asymmetries that can be 'read' visually by looking at the shape of the text on the page; type and negative space become a sonic map of sounds and silences, one that both embodies and interprets the textual content.

The final chapter of this book considers the idea of space as a language, from which we can infer the idea of a 'poetics of typographic space'. Any topic which involves relationships between 'inside' and 'outside' invites

[7] D. Crystal, 'Toward a Typographical Linguistics'. *Type*. 2 (1998), p. 13

[8] J. Drucker, 'Quantum Leap: Beyond Literal Materiality'. in M. Bierut,
      W. Drenttel, S. Heller (eds.), *Looking Closer 5* (New York: Allworth, 2006), p. 29

[9] A. de Campos, D. Pignatari, H. de Campos, *Pilot Plan for Concrete
      Poetry* (1958). Retrieved 25 October 2022, from https://ubu-mirror.ch/papers/
      noigandres01.html

wider interpretations. In his 1958 'The Poetics of Space' Gaston Bachelard refers to 'the dialectics of outside and inside'[10] and these concepts are not only fundamental to typography but also applicable across a variety of disciplines and contexts. In exploring these, the book will consider the common experience of typographic space within an expanded frame of reference, to locate this seemingly arcane design concept within a wider cultural perspective.

It should also be said that this book is a personal enquiry into ideas around the meaning of typographic space. As such it does not attempt to determine the means by which such space was calculated. Detailed work has been done on the measurements of typography; notably Peter Burnhill's investigation of the in-house norms of Aldus,[11] Frank Blokland's theories on the dimensions of the letters of the early typefounders,[12] and Andrew Boag's chronology of typographic measurement.[13] In his 1963 *Human Space* O. F. Bollnow makes an important distinction between mathematical space and human space,[14] and this has an equivalent in the reader's experience of typography; the eye traversing a page of text is not so much measuring the spaces as inhabiting them. It is necessary therefore to view typography not only through measurement but as a matter of human space. This space is experienced at several levels that interact with each other, and the conceptual structure of this book has been designed to examine these levels in order and reflect upon their individual and cumulative significance for both reader and designer.

[10] G. Bachelard, *The Poetics of Space*, Translated by M. Jolas (Boston: Beacon Press, 1994), p. 211

[11] P. Burnhill, *Type Spaces: In-house Norms in the Typography of Aldus Manutius* (London: Hyphen, 2003).

[12] F. Blokland, *On the Origin of Patterning in Movable Latin Type* (2016). Retrieved 25 October 2022, from https://hdl.handle.net/1887/43556

[13] A. Boag, 'Typographic Measurement: A Chronology'. in *Typography Papers*, 1 (University of Reading, 1996).

[14] O. F Bollnow, *Human Space*, Translated by C. Shuttleworth (London: Hyphen, 2011), p. 17

1 The Space within the Letter

This chapter will consider the nature and function of space within the designed letterform. The printed letter begins not in shapes but in spaces, created by the introduction of voids into a solid mass. Since the inception of printing from movable type in the mid-fifteenth century, the printer's letter has differed from those made by calligraphers, engravers, and sign-painters in one significant respect: it is a relief form rather than an autographic one, created by carving away rather than making a written or incised stroke. Unlike letters made by handwriting or engraving, the punches from which letters were originally cast were made by a subtractive process: a removal of their negative spaces. Where written letters are formed by the action of making a stroke, typographic letters are *fashioned* – a process of modelling or 'whittling' in which positive shape and space are developed in reference to each other. In the design of type, space and letter-shape must therefore be considered as interdependent parts rather than an active shape against a passive background: together, they form the 'ying' and 'yang' necessary to the whole. To design type is to engage in what Fred Smeijers, in his book *Counterpunch*, calls 'a game of black and white'[15] or Bachelard's 'dialectic of inner and outer'.[16] Like architecture, type design establishes complex relationships between interior and exterior, between mass and void, and gives purpose and meaning to the space it encloses.

1.1 Interior Shapes

The letter is assembled from spaces, either contained or open, with their own descriptive vocabulary. This includes the 'counter', a fully enclosed space as found within o, d, and p, and the smaller counter of the a, e, and g, sometimes referred to as the 'eye'. The wider term 'counterform' is commonly used to describe all the negative spaces within the overall shape of the letter, and therefore also includes the open spaces within c, n, m. These vary in 'aperture' – the opening from the counterform into the surrounding space – which may be wide or narrow. This leads to some ambiguities,

---

[15] F. Smeijers, *Counterpunch* (London: Hyphen, 2011), p. 24

[16] Bachelard, *The Poetics of Space*, p. 211

discussed in detail by Smeijers, as to whether a space is properly 'inside' a letter or part of its intercharacter space, which will be considered in Chapter 2.

For its first 500 years, type production involved the sculpting-away of metal from the face of the punch, and therefore involved unique considerations of 'inner' and 'outer', and the independence of interior profile from exterior profile marks a key distinction between the printer's letter and the calligraphic letter. Punch-cutting is a matter of visual subtraction; of punching-out and filing-away and the design and execution of the letter is a succession of visual decisions about the shapes of spaces. The interior shapes would be either carved out with a graver or more commonly punched out with a counterpunch – a tool specially fashioned for this purpose. Crucially, Smeijers locates this as the beginning of the punch-cutting process: the letter form actually starts from the design of its interior space, after which its outer profile is shaped to complete the resulting letter.[17] This explicitly demonstrates the active role of space as fundamental to the design process.

1.2 The Space and the Stroke

Since type originated as the mechanical expression of the manual practice of writing, it might be assumed that typographic shapes should be determined by the norms of handwriting. This is the view held by the Dutch graphic artist and educator Gerrit Noordzij, whose 'theory of the stroke' provides a robust design framework based upon the expansion and translation of the pen-stroke.[18] There is, however, no particular reason why the written hand should continue to dictate the aesthetic norms of type. Type is not writing, and while Noordzij's theories provide a persuasive and consistent formula for the making of a certain kind of letter, it is limited by the presumption of a direct equivalence between these practices, which have in fact been diverging for over 500 years. This is particularly significant with regard to the status of space in the letter-making process. In written letters

---

[17] Smeijers, *Counterpunch*, p. 79

[18] G. Noordzij, *The Stroke: Theory of Writing*, Translated by P. Enneson (London: Hyphen, 2005)

(distinguished by Smeijers as those in which 'each significant part is made of one stroke'), the space within the letter is an outcome, determined by autographic factors – the shape of the stroke and the width and angle of the tool used to create it. For the punch-cutter, the interior space was the first shape to be fashioned. This marks a very important distinction between the nature of space in typography and in the letter arts.

1.3 The Divergent Counterform

When interior space is considered as independent of the exterior profile (rather than as the by-product of the stroke), it presents new questions and stylistic possibilities. As type has evolved away from specific reference to calligraphic origins, the relationship between the interior and exterior space has become more complex. In his typefaces from the 1930s William Addison Dwiggins made dynamic use of the contrast or dissonance between the outer and inner profile. His practice of cutting stencils for many of the repeat elements of letters allowed the inner and outer profiles to be considered separately, creating an interior space that was independent of any common 'stroke'. The relationality of the letters is established through the repeated use of common shapes rather than the consistent action of a writing tool. The 'M-formula', by which he described this approach to typefaces such as *Electra*, allows for a controlled dissonance between the letter's exterior and interior profiles, introducing sharp angles into the interior curves to produce a 'whip-lash vitality'.[19] The M-formula was derived from observations of the action of light upon the features of carved marionettes, illuminating angled planes to give the impression of curves. This approach to the design of a letter's interior space is directly opposed to the stroke-based approach advocated by Noordzij. Divergence from the behaviour of the writing tool has also characterised the development of twentieth-century blackletter typefaces. While Rudolf Koch's *Kochschrift* clearly reflects the traditions of the idiom, he noted that its distinctiveness lies in the qualities that could not have been achieved with the pen-stroke alone, in the divergences between outer and inner space that animate and

[19] P. Shaw, 'W.A. Dwiggins: Jack of all Trades, Master of More Than One'. *Linotype Matrix*. 4.2. (2006), p. 45

enliven the letters.[20] The interior space of letters is also a key to stylistic differences between related typefaces; in many cases the differences are more evident in the interior spaces than the exterior profiles. This is clearly demonstrated in Martin Majoor's *Scala* and *Scala Sans*, an extended super-family that includes both serif and sans serif. Comparison of these designs reveals that the variations between them are most evident on the inside.

1.4 Drawing and the Letter

It is significant that Stanley Morison invited Eric Gill and others to 'draw letters' for Monotype rather than 'design typefaces';[21] though hand punch-cutting continued as a specialised practice into the mid-twentieth century, from the late nineteenth century it had been superseded by methods that allowed for larger drawings to be mechanically transcribed to punches or matrices. This had the significant effect of opening up the field of type production to the input of graphic artists, sculptors, and architects, redefining the relationship between type design and drawing. As Smeijers observes, drawing a letter in outline describes a contour which does not present a form, but only defines its border or edge.[22] It has the effect of deferring any consideration of space relationships until the outline has been filled. He also contrasts a drawing 'made in one go' with the development of a letter starting first with the creation of the counters 'as is the case with cutting text sizes in metal'[23] – a sequence of shape development that differs radically from making an outline drawing. The transition from outline to silhouette will normally involve both positive and negative processes; as important as the 'inking-in' will be the revisions made with process white or gouache; a subtractive process like the punch-cutter's. Type designers' drawings from the era of machine composition often reveal this 'whiting-out', and this aspect of the letter design process is more than simply the correcting of errors; it is the drawing and refining of the letter's negative space.

[20] G. Cinamon, *Rudolf Koch: Letterer, Type Designer, Teacher* (London: British Library, 2000), p. 26

[21] R. Kinross, *Modern Typography* (London: Hyphen, 1994), p. 62

[22] Smeijers, *Counterpunch*, p. 18

[23] Cinamon, *Rudolf Koch: Letterer, Type Designer, Teacher*, p. 92

1.5 The Subtractive Letter

The use of typographic space in the letter arts reflects cultural differences and variations of stylistic tradition. Architectural lettering and monumental inscriptions in Central Europe show a tradition of relief lettering largely without equivalent in Britain. The raised letter is created subtractively, like the punch, and it is by the cutting-away of stone that the recognisable form of the letter emerges. British inscriptional lettering, by contrast, has after its early vernacular origins centred upon the incised letter: writing with a chisel. In this more 'Roman' approach, the space is a surface into which the letter is incised, and the negative space is a result of this mark-making process. In relief lettercutting, however, the space is the medium by which the letter is formed. This difference in vernacular craft traditions would seem to correspond to the contrasting print cultures of roman and black-letter type. In the nineteenth and twentieth centuries, as an increasing variety of novel forms entered the world of type production from graphic and vernacular traditions, the subtractive display letterform manifests in print and the preeminent examples are Central European. Rudolf Koch's *Neuland* is explicitly subtractive, created directly through punchcutting. Gerald Cinamon affirms that 'much of the character is due to the variety and inventiveness created by the designer himself guiding the punch-cutting tool'.[24] The work of Rudolf von Larisch is also significant here since he rejected the blackletter tradition and placed particular significance on the proportion of space between letters, to the extent of giving greater importance to the distribution of space than the letter shape itself. Nash and Williams note that his alphabets 'emphasized the figure-ground relation between the letter and the writing surface'.[25] The subtractive lettering of Koloman Moser and Alfred Roller typified the graphic styles of the Vienna

---

[24] R. Nash, R. Williams, *Revival of Calligraphy (19th and 20th Centuries)* (2000). Retrieved 25 October 2022, from www.britannica.com/art/calligraphy/Revival-of-calligraphy-19th-and-20th-centuries

[25] K. Thomas, 'Rudolf von Larisch: Investigating and Analysing the Ideas and Theories of a Lettering Reformer', unpublished Master's thesis, Monash University (2015), p. ii

Secession, and Roller in particular was to take this ideal to its extreme in letters that were essentially solid rectangles, into which the finest of linear incursions serve to identify the letter. These ideas were to be revisited in the work of Victor Moscoso and other American poster artists of the late 1960s.

1.6 Bold Fonts and Space

Alongside the advent of sans serif types, two key developments of late-nineteenth-century type design were the design of increasingly bold faces and the concept of multiple weights and widths within extended type families. Developing the additional weights of a typeface will inevitably have an impact upon the volume of negative space in their counterforms. A simple uniform increase of stroke weight will diminish the interior space, and for this reason the bold weights of many typefaces show a compensatory variation of stroke thickness; the weight is increased more in the vertical strokes than in the horizontals, giving greater contrast is in the bold weights than the regular. This can lead to noticeable differences of style between the weights of the same typeface.

1.7 Ascender and Descender Space

The shape of spaces within characters is central to the analysis of their legibility. It is widely recognised that high ascenders assist word-shape recognition.[26] The 'ascender space' from x-height to ascender height and the 'descender space' from baseline to the depth of the descender vary considerably from one typeface to another. The inbuilt space above the lowercase letter with high ascenders is therefore deeper and faces designed for book setting are characterised by more pronounced ascenders designed for generous leading, a topic that will be examined in Chapter 4. An important feature in character recognition is the space at the junctions, where curved strokes join stems (as in b,h,n,d) and studies have established that deep junctions aid letter recognition and legibility.[27]

---

[26] S. Beier, *Reading Letters: Designing for Legibility* (Amsterdam: Bis, 2012)
[27] ibid.

1.8 Space and the Serif

The function of space in punch-cutting provides us with a unique perspective not only on the counter and counterform, but also on the widely debated status of the serif. Serifs are a key aspect of the exterior profile of the letter, and the following chapter will consider their impact upon inter-character space, but they also determine the shape of the counterform, typically in letters such as H, h, X, and are therefore a feature of the interior space of serif letters. From the punchcutter's perspective the serif would be inherent in the shaping of negative space around the letter profile, rather than an extraneous mark added to the 'stroke'. Drawing a letter in outline, it will be natural for the designer to first establish the main strokes, then add the serif as a further detail. If, however, a letter is being cut from the outside, the serif will be formed as part of a single and continuous subtractive profile.

1.9 Conclusion

As we have seen, the interior space of letters is an indivisible part of their form, and has since the inception of movable type been fashioned independently of the written 'stroke'. Smeijers's 'game of black and white' has no direct equivalent in handwriting, and thus defines some qualities particular to the typographic letter, that originate in the processes of punchcutting and continue into present-day digital design. The complex relationship between these interior spaces and the space between letters will be considered in the next chapter.

2 The Space between Letters

After examining the spaces within letters, we are able then to consider the spaces between them. This chapter will examine the significance of inter-character spacing in both practical and aesthetic terms, looking at the variety of different methods and approaches by which it has been measured, and the way in which these align to different design philosophies.

It is the properties of intercharacter space which distinguish type from lettering or writing. This is expressed with particular rigour by Smeijers, who locates the defining characteristic of type (and the difference between type and lettering) not in the repetition of identical letter-forms, but in consistent mechanical systems of letter spacing.[28] This feature, unique to typography, requires the development of systematic methods within the type production process. The practical parameters for such a method are that spaces should be open enough to distinguish the letters, but close enough to maintain the gestalt of a unified 'word image'. Established aesthetic ideals are an appearance of equal space between all letters, and that both interior space and intercharacter space should provide an even 'rhythm' of dark and light.

Current practice in the design of type involves not only designing shapes but regularising the space-relationships between these shapes. Any attempt to simply insert identical spaces between the extremities of every letter will quickly reveal that letters require different amounts of space for the letter-spacing to appear consistent, and any designer who has completed a type design to production will confirm that the design of a letter's inherent spacing is a complex and demanding aspect of this process. In particular, the nature of a letter's interior space and its profile will determine the amount of intercharacter space it requires. This distinction between interior space and intercharacter space proves, however, to be less absolute than we might suppose. While straight-sided capitals offer clear boundaries between letter and space, this distinction is immediately compromised by letters with open counterforms, one of the factors that undermines any attempt to impose a consistent measurement between the

---

[28] Smeijers, *Counterpunch*, p. 21

extremities of a letter. The space between letters is composed both of counterform and inter-character space. Willem Sandberg's work uses the resulting negative shapes as visual entities in their own right, like jigsaw pieces linking the letters together, an idea developed and given further practical application in Cyrus Highsmith's small and illuminating book *Inside Paragraphs*.[29] Smeijers explains the variables in these terms: 'If we insert a character with an open counter, we soon discover that there is no clear border between the space that belongs to the inner area of the character and the space that belongs to the area between the two characters.' He continues: 'The way to resolve this is to understand that a certain part of the adjoining space has a double function. This area is inner-space and outer space at the same time.'[30] These observations serve to confirm the complexity of determining the character spacing as an integral aspect of typeface design.

2.1 Intercharacter Space in Letter Design

In view of the significant relationship between spaces within the letter and the spaces between, it is understandable that the contemporary type designer views the intercharacter spacing as integral to a letter's design. As we have seen, typographic norms are informed by type production history. The cast metal sort was a material form derived from the material processes of punchcutting, and this form included the whole body, including the unprinted 'shoulder' or 'fitting space', as a three-dimensional solid. The letter space is therefore a material part of the designed object, and the design of type determines the space-relationships that occur between the letters. This is affirmed by Walter Tracy in his *Letters of Credit*, where he makes the point that design of the inter-character space is an integral part of the type design process, since it determines 'the overall texture of the type en masse'.[31]

---

[29] C. Highsmith, *Inside Paragraphs: Typographic Fundamentals* (Newyork: Princeton Architectural Press, 2020)

[30] Smeijers, *Counterpunch*, pp. 30–2

[31] W. Tracy, *Letters of Credit* (Boston: Godine, 1986), p. 71

In his *Detail in Typography*, Jost Hochuli defines the space between letters as a 'function' of their interior spaces, concluding that the smaller the counter, the smaller the space needed between letters. He supports this with the observation that letter-spacing that appears lighter than the median lightness of the counters of the letters compromises the 'word-image'.[32] This serves to further affirm the reciprocal nature of interior and intercharacter spaces. The literature of design education often refers to balancing 'equal areas' of inter-character space. In *Typographic Design: Form and Communication* Carter, Day and Meggs quote Ben Shahn's account of advice given to him as an apprentice: 'Imagine that you have in your hand a glass that will hold only so much water. Now you must provide space between your letters – whatever their slants or curves may be – to hold just that much water, no more or less.'[33] They then make an important distinction in identifying the need to make the interlinear space *appear* equal, and go on to say, 'Because these counterform spaces have such different configurations, this spacing must be achieved through optical balance rather than through measurement' since a balance of mathematical area alone does not provide for evenness of appearance. The limits of mathematical 'balance' are further affirmed by Hochuli when he refers to an example from Tschichold, saying that 'although the areas between the letters are not equal, the word appears evenly spaced. So this cannot be a matter of spaces of equal area'.[34] Hochuli's solution to is to 'replace the concept of area with that of light', which he asserts 'flows from above and below into the interior spaces of the letters and the space between them'. The light coming from above, he asserts, is 'more effective' than that coming from below. 'This means that the n of a sanserif typeface must be somewhat wider than the u of the same typeface.'[35] While his concept of 'light' may not be as self-evident as he implies, this is significant in suggesting that a letter spacing

---

[32] J. Hochuli, *Detail in Typography* (Montreuil: Éditions B42, 2015), p. 22

[33] R. Carter, B. Day, P. Meggs, *Typographic Design: Form and Communication* (Hoboken: Wiley, 2006), p. 51

[34] Hochuli, *Detail in Typography*, pp. 25–7 [35] ibid.

problem may be addressed by modifying the letter design. Tracy notes that 'The fitting of the alphabets is best done when the letters have been sketched but before they are finished, because the fitting process may require adjustments of the character widths'.[36] This affirms that a fully integrated process of type design involves interdependent decisions over letter profile and the surrounding space, in which each may be modified by reference to the other.

The Serif and Intercharacter Space

Much of the debate among type designers and historians concerning the serif has focused upon whether it is extraneous or fundamental to the structure of the letter, or to its supposed function in 'directing' the eye along the line. Less attention has been given to its impact upon letter-spacing. While Pacioli, Durer and de Tory's drawings did not attempt to apply concepts of 'divine proportion' to the spaces *between* letter shapes, it is notable that all include the serif as a part of the letter's overall width, and as therefore essential to the inference of a universal geometric principle. The serif has the effect of moderating the contrast between letters with straight sides and those with open counterforms: the upright of a serif letter is rendered as a very shallow open shape by the serif at its foot and head. The design of serif letters therefore provides for a greater conformity of visual rhythm than is possible with sans serifs. Burnhill suggests that in the cutting of punches for early typefounders, the serifs could function as consistent units of spacing for casting evenly close-spaced lowercase characters.[37] The design of type addresses the relationship between the letter's interior space and the space between the letters, and in this context, the serif can be seen not as a stylistic addition to the stroke, but as a key element in the counterform and thus of the inter-character space. As the principle of consistent rhythm depends upon a correspondence between these two, the serif can be seen as a defining feature shaping the inter-character space, rather than an extraneous ornament. It serves to mediate the space difference between straight and round-sided letters.

[36] Tracy, *Letters of Credit*, p. 72
[37] Burnhill, *Type spaces: In-house Norms in the Typography of Aldus Manutius*, p. 66

Spacing Capitals

Writers on typography agree that when capital letters are set to form whole words or sentences, the spacing should be increased. If simply set to the normal spacing intervals necessary for a good fit with lower case letters, strings of capitals will appear both optically dense and uneven. In *The Form of the Book* Tschichold states that 'roman capital letters must always and under all circumstances be letterspaced, using a minimum of one-sixth their body size'.[38] Furthermore, the integrity of the word shape as a visual unit is less significant in these instances than it would be in continuous lower-case text, and words set as capitals may be read letter-by-letter; a quality that may be underlined by exaggerated letter-spacing. This aids the distinction between the running text and capitalised features such as titles or running heads. Anthony Froshaug devised a detailed table of spacing values for capital letters in 1945, in a text titled 'The Field of a Majuscule'.[39] This was never implemented and remained unpublished until 1975, at which time he noted the impact of photosetting in compounding the problems he had identified.

Letter Space for Emphasis

The use of letter spacing as a medium of emphasis has deep roots in typographic history and is particularly associated with the Germanic black-letter. The blackletter tradition has no clear equivalent to the distinction between upright and Italic that developed within the early development of roman type, while relatively heavy weights and high contrasts offered limited scope for the development of bold variants. Tschichold states, 'In Fraktur, letterspacing is used to set words off from their neighbours. Formerly one used a different type as well, Schwabacher for example'.[40] Letter-spacing or *Sperrung* remained the dominant method of emphasis and differentiation in Germany, where blackletter continued to be widely used for literary texts up to the mid-twentieth century. It is also found in Polish and Cyrillic typesetting. This use of space creates emphasis by moderating

---

[38] J. Tschichold, *The Form of the Book* (London: Lund Humphries, 1991), p. 44

[39] A. Froshaug, 'The Field of a Majuscule'. In R. Kinross (ed.), *Anthony Froshaug Typography and Texts* (London: Hyphen, 2000), p. 211

[40] Tschichold, *The Form of the Book*, p. 44

the speed of reading, rather than the increased 'volume' achieved by bold type or the visual surprise of a different typeface. The word as visual unit is deliberately broken into its component parts, requiring the reader to read letter by letter. The space between the letters becomes a rhetorical device, in inviting the reader to 'spell out' particular words, recalling the unspaced words of the 'scripta continua' which will be discussed in Chapter 3.

2.2 Visual Rhythm

The term 'visual rhythm' is used to describe the pattern of alternating dark and light in a line of type. This pattern is determined not simply by the intervals between letters, but by the relationships between the spaces within letters and the spaces between them. An even visual rhythm therefore requires balanced volumes of interior space and inter-character space. Tracy quotes Harry Carter: 'The success or failure of a type is very much a question of getting a good balance of white inside and outside the letters.'[41] The need to maintain this balance is a defining criterion in type design. Gutenberg's *Textura* type was derived from a scribal hand distinguished by the rhythmic correspondence of interior and exterior typographic space; the concept of 'texture' denoting an even-ness of rhythm. This quality is inherent in the forms of the letters, as the space between the vertical strokes that make up the letters determines the space between them; the form of the letter has clearly evolved to this end. The Roman letter, however, offers no such exact correspondence; letter profiles and apertures vary dramatically from one letter to the next, each requiring different approaches to the inter-character spacing of the letter in question. In practice the design of a font involves very detailed attention to the metrics, a term that includes two key concepts: sidebearings and kerning.

Sidebearings

The sidebearing is the name given to the 'fitting space' space to left and right of the letter. The concept is perhaps best summarised by Dwiggins in his letter of 1940 to Rudolf Ruzika:[42]

---

[41] Tracy, *Letters of Credit*, p. 71 [42] ibid. p. 72

Each type letter, wherever it goes, carries along with it two *fixed* blank spaces, one on either side. And of course, each one of the 26 is likely to be placed alongside any one of the other 25 with their fixed blank spaces ... The letter shapes occur in groups of similar: when you have solved for n alongside of n you are close to a workout for h I j l m and for the stem sides of b d k p q – a proper fitting for o gives you a line on the round shapes ... a, c, e on their open sides, and f g r t are hard to fit.

In the typefounding process of metal types from the fifteenth to the nineteenth centuries, we can already see the space between characters as an integral part of the letter's design. The 'dressing' of the matrix included a minimal provision of space on either side of the letter.[43] The resulting 'sort' therefore defined not only the letter's shape but the minimum amount of space on either side. This space is not only an integral element of the letter's visual design, but a material part of its solid form. It could be increased – laboriously by the insertion of spacing between the sorts – but it could not be reduced (except by kerning, as described below)

Kerning

In addition to the variations in sidebearing value, certain problematic letter pairs will require particular adjustments to the letter space between them. Typical examples would be the capitals A V and T A. In hand-set metal type these necessitated shaving away metal from the sides of some sorts to achieve a better fit. In digital typography this involves programming revised spacing values to override the normal sidebearings of a letter when it occurs in particular 'problem' letter-pairs; an automated 'smart' feature that is an inherent part of the typeface design process. A digital font designed to professional standards may involve a large number of kern pairs. While this varies widely according to the design, there are about 100 letter pairs (or pairings of letters and punctuation marks) that can commonly by expected to require kerning. Kerning is necessitated by the shapes of particular letter profiles in combination, and the need for kerning may

---

[43] ibid.

instead be addressed by the designer at source, by moderating the shapes of the letters to minimise those problems that would otherwise require kerning as their solution. This is a further area in which the type designer may address a spacing problem by revising the design, affirming the inter-dependence of form and space within the design process.

2.3 Divergent Approaches: The Printing Trade and the Letter Arts

The interior space of a letter is closely interdependent with the spacing it requires, and for the early punchcutter and typefounder, the space around the letter was an indivisible part of its material substance. The successive technologies of mechanised typecasting and photosetting were to separate these qualities, while developments in the letter arts provided different perspectives on the nature of inter-character space.

The early twentieth century marks a divergence between the industrialisation of type production methods and the conscious 'revival' of craft practices of lettering, one which becomes particularly evident with regard to spacing methods. Two key examples reveal not only a significant difference of approach, but an underlying cultural divide between the letter crafts and the printing trade.

Edward Johnston's Spacing Rules

In his paper *Edward Johnston and Letter Spacing*,[44] Colin Banks looks at the spacing of letters designed by a highly regarded letter-craftsman whose understanding of *typographic* space and form can be seen to be relatively uninformed. Unlike metal types, display-sized wooden types normally have no inbuilt spacing but extend to the full width of the wood block. Spacing was therefore carried out by hand, by the compositor or signmaker, and it was for this purpose that Johnston formulated a set of spacing rules. Like his pupil and successor Eric Gill, Johnston seems to have considered his own visual judgement to be more relevant to the task in hand than any reference to existing trade knowledge. As Banks has noted, the table of spacing he devised depends upon the conjunction of shapes of neighbouring letters but

---

[44] C. Banks, 'Edward Johnston and Letter Spacing'. In J. Berry, J. Randle (eds.), *Type and Typography* (New York: Mark Batty, 2003), p. 347

does not allow for variations in the interior space within each letter, a factor historically addressed by punchcutters and summarised later by Tracy. It seems that an ideological prejudice against the printing trade and unexamined faith in the craftsman's hand predisposed Johnston to ignore this. As Banks notes, he was 'curiously unaware or wilfully indifferent to'[45] the preceding 500 years of typographic knowledge and seems to have assumed that his experience of the positioning of calligraphic letters would be adequate to the application of space within typographic design. Specification of typographic space was an aspect of the design process that Johnston and Gill may have been less fully equipped to address than they supposed. Tracy notes: 'Eric Gill, for instance, who from his experience as an inscriptional letter-cutter had an expert sense of the spacing of characters, was content to say, in a letter to Stanley Morrison about a proof of trials of Perpetua Roman 'the space between letters wants alteration, but as you say, that can be done independently of me.'[46] Tracy may be generous to Gill in assuming that his understanding of sequential letter-cutting would have equipped him to determine the fitting of type. Morison may have wanted to avoid involving Gill in detailed argument over the matter, and to have understood that inscriptional letter-cutting and typeface design involve two very different ways of looking at space.

David Kindersley and the 'Optical Centre'

Similar craft-based conceptions of typographic spacing inform the work of the lettercutter David Kindersley, who from the 1950s through the 1980s developed an approach to letter spacing based upon locating and balancing the 'optical centres' of letters.

Kindersley's system suggests the perspective of a letter craftsman rather than a typographer. By his own account it originates in some observations on street signs composed wholly of capitals, and, like Johnston, he depends upon the authority of personal experience without recourse to existing industry knowledge. He states rather that 'Our aim has been to find out how the eye assesses the character's space which was done so easily by the

---

[45] ibid. p. 349 [46] Tracy, *Letters of Credit*, pp. 71–2

early professional scribe'.[47] It is revealing that he should refer here to scribal tradition rather than any example of excellence in printing, and his approach provides another example of original thinking developed independent of the accumulated knowledge of trade or industry. Never adopted into type production, his theory is noteworthy less as a practical solution than as a different way of thinking about the problem.

Kindersley's system reflects a background in the practice of lettercutting in stone, and indicates that beyond the common concern for some consistent visual rhythm, intercharacter space within the letter crafts involves different considerations. The letter artist's space is consequent, while the type designer's space is intrinsic. For the sign-writer, calligrapher, or lettercutter, the intercharacter space is uniquely formed within the process of making each successive letter and is not a material part of the letter's design – only of its implementation. Though calligraphers such as Mahoney, Camp, and Waters have formulated the ideals of even spacing in terms similar to type designers, the application of these principles involves a quite different method of appending space to the letter. In a practice that involves forming a line of successive letters, the forward bearing or advance space to the right of the letter will necessarily be the more significant. Having made one letter, we can consider the space between its right-facing extremities and those of the succeeding letter (we cannot read-back the left-hand space of a letter that has not yet been made). By comparison the type designer, designing letters independently of their application, can give equal consideration to the space on both sides, at left and right of the letters. The resulting spacing may be very similar and reflect the same visual values, but the means by which it is achieved is conceptually different.

Spacing and Twentieth-Century Type Technologies

In fairness, Kindersley's initiative should be viewed in its historical context. In the later phases of the brief interval between the technologies of metal and digital type, photosetting enabled letters input from a keyboard to be electronically stored, before being distributed along the line in an evenly balanced manner. For a short while therefore it seemed it might be no

[47] D. Kindersley, 'LOGOS: Letterspacing with a Computer'. In D. Jury (ed.), *Typographic Writing* (Stroud: ISTD, 2001), p. 174

longer necessary to consider a letter as having an inherent letter space at all, and Kindersley in 1983 anticipates that the 'new printing systems' would provide for automated and variable spacing independent of input from the type designer, and states that 'One is now free from spacing letters within rectangles'.[48] His system is therefore peculiar to the period of technological history in which it was devised, in that it is fully immaterial and anticipates the development of letter-spacing as an independent system of machine parameters, rather than a part of the letter's design. This occurred at a point when photosetting technology was reaching new levels of sophistication, but before conventions of specification had been standardised for digital type design. These were in fact to return more closely to the original model of metal type, establishing that digital letters should have predetermined sidebearings analogous to those of a metal sort. Douglas Martin, in his 1989 *An Outline of Book Design*, notes a key point in this development, while also observing the similarities between the approach taken in Peter Karow's *Digital Formats for Typefaces* and the *Romain du Roi*. He says, 'It is perhaps inevitable, but nevertheless reassuring, that the raster used in digitisation is firmly linked to the printer's traditional system of measurement; to quote Dr Karow "We [at UKW] are of the opinion that describing a letter according to its em is the best way of picturing the digitisation of type".'[49] In this development, digital design resolves the rift between design of space and design of letter which had begun with the production workflow of types for mechanical composition and diverged further with developments in photosetting.

2.4 Aesthetic Values and User Expectations

Attempting a single standard for spacing reveals a tension between two established principles. On the one hand, we have established that a letter's internal space is integral to its form, and that differences between letters are the basis for their recognition, a point explored and demonstrated by Hrant Papazian in his essay *Improving the Tool*.[50] The resulting 'difference'

[48] ibid.

[49] D. Martin, *An Outline of Book Design* (London: Blueprint, 1989), p. 43

[50] H. Papazian, 'Improving the Tool'. In G. Swanson, (ed.), *Graphic Design and Reading* (New York: Allworth, 2000), pp. 125–6

is therefore one of space as well as shape. Its practical value therefore contradicts the formal principles of 'equal volume' and 'even rhythm'.

While it would be simplistic to advance one of these opposing considerations over the other, they exist in an unresolved relationship, one moreover that varies widely according to the characteristics of the typeface. The 'glass of water' method therefore represents a contributory perspective on letter spacing rather than an absolute rule. While inter-character space and internal space may be considered as one fluid substance, they represent two different orders of function – though the boundaries are permeable, as Smeijers has shown.[51] In our visual interpretation of text, the space that is *part* of a letter clearly has a semantic function and value different from the space *between* letters, and to treat these as the same material is to substitute abstract formal concerns for practical ones – a familiar and recurrent lapse in modernist design thinking. The limits of this approach can be demonstrated through one of the common 'problem pairs' of letters: the capitals LT. Unless the string of capitals has been quite dramatically letter-spaced overall, the space created by the voids of these two letters in combination will be much greater than the spaces between other letters. If the letter pairs are kerned until the volume of white space between them and adjacent letters is *equal* to that in other letter-pairs (applying the principle of Shahn's glass of water), the horizontal strokes of each letter would intrude into the internal space of the other. While the resulting rather mannered effect might be acceptable in a piece of custom lettering, lettercutting or calligraphy, such kerning would be intrusive in printed type.

The Indesign programme released by Adobe in 1999 introduced an 'optical kerning' feature, which overrides the kerning values determined by the font's designer, to give instead an 'optically balanced' space between letters. It is a measure of the significance placed upon kerning as an integral aspect of contemporary typeface design that some independent type foundries actively discouraged its use, while discriminating type users observed that the trust we place in a designer or foundry should apply as much to the quality of kerning as to the letter design itself. The amount of resulting deviation from the inbuilt metrics varies quite widely between typefaces. When applied to traditional faces that originate in metal type, optical

---

[51] Smeijers, *Counterpunch*, pp. 30–2

kerning reveals an unexpected and very subtle dissonance. This might be explained in two related ways. The first is that our user expectations of printed letters are still informed by historic norms. Letters originally created within the very limited kerning options offered by metal type were designed to provide a satisfactory result under less than ideal conditions of production and reproduction. The inter-character space we associate with these letters reflects the constraints of the technology in which they originated and is part of the design, not only for the designer but for the reader. The expectations of a reader familiar with those serif roman letters which still account for the majority of long-text setting will reflect the spacing we associate with these letters from their original context as hand-set or machine-composed metal type. Apart from a very limited use of kerns and ligatures, the spacing of these letters reflects the constraints of their production; each letter is set upon a rectangular body and designed to be assembled in sequence. The voids below the crossbar of the T or to the right of the stem of the L have become inherent and irreducible parts of the shape that we recognise. The space within the metal letter was a designed part of the body, determined by the designer or punchcutter, while adjustment to the spacing of particular letter-pairs was a post-production process by the compositor. This affirms again that are dealing with two interdependent, but distinct, types of space, rather than the single unifying concept of 'area' (or indeed Hochuli's 'light'). At a more fundamental level we can consider the 'idea' of the letter, independent of typographic conventions, and arrive at similar conclusions. The idea of the 'L-shape' or 'T-shape' comprises both the stroke and the void defined by it. As we have seen in Chapter 1, the normative form of these and indeed all letters is composed of both shape and space. A capital L is composed not only of two right-angled shapes but also the void they create above the horizontal. Our user-expectation of the letter includes this void as an essential element in the recognition of its form, and the volume of space we associate with the letter in this way varies considerably from one letter to another.

User expectation is not of course fixed or absolute. It evolves, often over a very long cycle, and digital type design provides at least one instance in which norms may begin to shift. One recent example addresses a problem in the optical properties of the capital T, when combined with lowercase ascender letters. The designer Robert Slimbach, responsible for many of the highly regarded text typefaces produced by the Adobe corporation, favours a Th ligature, to such an extent that it occurs as a default ligature in many of his typefaces. This composite letter is 'retrofitted' to Adobe's digital adaptations of 'classic' types including Caslon, Garamond, and Jenson. The admitted elegance of this anomalous and a-historical form combines with the sheer reach and influence of a producer like Adobe to suggest that it will in time probably become an accepted norm.

2.5 Conclusion

As professional problem-solvers, designers are particularly susceptible to the attractions of systems and formulae, and to the notion that 'rules' or 'laws' might be derived from them. The superficial appeal of a unifying concept offered by Shahn's glass of water, Kindersley's optical centre, or the Adobe Optical Kerning system must in practice be mediated by a sensitivity to normative form and user expectation. The idea of 'equalising' or 'balancing' space is an essentially abstract notion that has taken on the authority of convention, and its aesthetic merits require an equal regard for the semantic properties of the letter; properties that depend upon the interaction of shape and space as integral in the process of letter recognition. The 'glass of water' idea therefore represents just one of several contributory perspectives on letter spacing which need to be considered concurrently and synthesised according to the context in which they are being applied. As a practical ideal, spacing should not disturb the eye or disrupt the reading experience; and these considerations are informed by cultural factors of user expectation as much as abstract notions of optical balance. The contrasting approaches of Johnston and Kindersley further afform that approaches to space reflect different cultural values as well as responding to shifts in technological perspective.

Finally: Hochuli's argument for 'sufficient close fit' has a clear practical implication for the recognition of the word shape, and demonstrates the interdependence of letter-space with word-space, which we will consider in the next chapter.

3 Spaces between Words

Having examined space first as an element that defines the structure of letters, and then as the means by which they are connected to form words, we can now consider how this same element functions as the means by which words are separated from each other. This chapter will consider the origin, purpose, and significance of the word-space, before then looking at the ways in which word-space may be varied in response to wider design decisions at the discretion of the typographer.

According to the widely established 'parallel letter recognition model' the letters within a word are recognised simultaneously, and the letter information is used to recognise the words.[52] Anthony Froshaug states that 'A word is a complete whole, a gestalt, as a constellation is something more than or other than the sum of its component stars'[53] and the function of the word-space is to visually distinguish these constellations from each other. This space is therefore a signifier, rather than simply a break between signifiers. (Saussure's concept of 'signifier' is 'made up of speech sounds', and speech sounds can no more exist without their corelative silence than letters can exist without counterforms.) We may also consider ancient Roman conventions of denoting word breaks by a median dot or interpunct (a form consciously revived for historical effect by designers of the nineteenth century) and view the word-space as a replacement for this; as a 'silent' letter, a designed void rather than an absence, an invisible correlative to the visible sounded letter. It is a 'non-visible symbol', denoting a period of silence or 'non-sound', just as a letter denotes a sound. This becomes particularly significant for the poet or playwright, as these spaces can be multiplied, in typewritten text and subsequently in print, to typographically represent controlled measures of silence: the 'structural agent' of concrete poetry as defined by the

---

[52] K. Larson, *The Science of Word Recognition* (2022). Retrieved 25 October 2022, from https://docs.microsoft.com/en-us/typography/develop/word-recognition

[53] A. Froshaug, 'On Typography'. In R. Kinross (ed.), *Anthony Froshaug Typography and Texts* (London: Hyphen, 2000), p. 108

Noigandres poets in the 1958 *Pilot Plan for Concrete Poetry*.[54] This idea
was explored by writers and artists of the twentieth-century European
avant-garde through the graphic structure of poems, graphic scores, or
libretti in which word-space is varied to denote duration of silence,
a topic we will return to in Chapter 7.

The word-space has more in common with the counterforms within
letters, than with the spaces between them, as it is a readable void with
a fixed and recognised meaning. It might even be described as a letter
composed wholly of counterform – a useful paradox analogous to the
Hindu 'Anahata Nada' or 'unstruck', or indeed the Zen 'sound of one
hand clapping'.

3.1 Historical Background

Early writing made no visual differentiation between words at all; the *scripta
continua* of classic Greek and Roman manuscripts is primarily a transcrip-
tion of the spoken word, to act as script or libretto for spoken transmission.
As Saenger affirms, the introduction of word-spaces and the consequent
'aerated' text first seen in the Irish and Anglo-Saxon Bibles and Gospels
from the seventh and eighth centuries reflects a significant cultural change in
context and method, from reading aloud to 'silent' reading.[55] Prior to word-
spacing, the oral 'reader' would be expected to construct the words within
the act of reading, and any sentence breaks or punctuation would be implicit
in this activity. Letter-spacing in the *scripta continua* would also be wider
than in the later word-spaced manuscripts. Letter-spacing was therefore
revised in the light of word-spacing, establishing an interdependent relationship between the letter-spacing of words and the volume of space
between them, and it is from this point that we can trace the word as
a coherent visual unit.

[54] A. de Campos, D. Pignatari, H. de Campos, *Pilot Plan for Concrete Poetry* (1958).
Retrieved 25 October 2022, from https://ubu-mirror.ch/papers/noigandres01
.html

[55] P. Saenger, *Space Between Words: The Origins of Silent Reading* (Redwood City:
Stanford University Press, 2000)

Smeijers identifies word-spacing as a defining feature of typography since the composition of the word is 'regulated by machine-fabrication'.[56] He describes the hand-printer's composing-stick as 'an elementary machine' through which the system extends beyond the word, to the line and the whole column. The mechanics of printing from movable type involved a standardisation of word-spacing, and examples of early printing show a common tendency to establish minimum spaces. Martin makes the point that Gutenberg and the early printers must have taken their priorities from an analysis of the best features of the manuscripts which they were setting out to rival and supplant,[57] while Geoffrey Dowding, in his *Finer Points in the Spacing and Arrangement of Type*, observes that the best work of the most famous printers since the mid-fifteenth century indicates that 'when words are set for continuous reading they should always be closely spaced',[58] and early printed books show word spacing far tighter than we would expect today, with no adverse effects on the readability of the text. Burnhill's study of the books published by Aldus Manutius in the late fifteenth and early sixteenth century includes the observation that within a paragraph, matter to be discussed is preceded by a large space.[59]

3.2 Word Unit and Line Unit

The typographer organises the relationships between words as groups of letters and lines as groups of words, and these are interdependent factors in the overall composition of the text. Dowding observes that Jenson's work 'illustrates how consistently close spacing between the words, and after the full points, secures one of the essentials of well set text matter – a strip like quality of line' and states that 'whenever word-spacing is increased beyond the thin space care must be taken not to increase it to the point where the line ceases to be a unit',[60] highlighting the reciprocity of word-space and

---

[56] Smeijers, *Counterpunch*, p. 21 [57] Martin, *An Outline of Book Design*, p. 28

[58] G. Dowding, *Finer Points in the Spacing and Arrangement of type* (London: Wace, 1954), p. 3

[59] Burnhill, *Type Spaces: In-house Norms in the Typography of Aldus Manutius*, p. 49

[60] Dowding, *Finer Points in the Spacing and Arrangement of Type*, p. 2

line-space. Charles Rosner's account of the house style of Balding and Mansell defines the purpose of a word-space as 'to divide a sentence into units of words, but not to separate them so much that they cease to become integral parts of the next largest unit, the line'.[61] The 'gestalt' or 'constellation' by which Froshaug defines the word requires not only differentiation from its individual components but also from adjacent constellations, including those in the lines above or below it.

The letterpress printer Paul Ritscher actually suggests that the word spacing should be determined by the leading, advising the designer/printer to 'space the words in relation to the leading that you are using'.[62] However, decisions on leading are more commonly governed by word spacing, derived in turn from the design and size of the type.

3.3 Systems of Spacing

While letter spacing can be most fully understood as an integral part of the letter's design, the word-space is an independent unit applicable to a variety of different type styles, and systems of word spacing reflect the constraints of the technologies of print production.

The nature of metal type as a mechanical system required a range of spaces to be cast for each size of type. In order for a common spacing system be applied consistently at each size, type spaces have therefore been traditionally expressed as fractions (or multiples) of the body size or em. The em is relative measurement; a space equal in width to the body height of the type, and the square em-quad is a primary unit, from which a set of standard spaces can be derived. The Monotype and Linotype systems of machine composition standardised word-spacing practices that had been established to varying degrees across the print culture of the preceding 400 years. Burnhill quotes Southward's *Modern Printing: A Handbook*:

[61] C. Rosner, *Type: Principles and Application* (Wisbech: Balding and Mansell, 1953), p. 19

[62] P. Ritscher, *Hand Setting*. Retrieved 25 October 2022, from www.briarpress.org/37356

Spaces, in width, are aliquot parts of the em unit of a fount.
There are five spaces generally supplied [by type founders] –
the en quad, the thick space, the middle space, the thin space,
and the hair space, thus:

En quad1/2 of the em, or 2 to em;

Thick space1/ 3 of the em, or 3 to em

Middle space1/4 of the em, or 4 to em;

Thin space = 1/5 of the em, or 5to em.

The hair space varies according to the size of the body.
In the smaller founts it is 1/10 of the em; in some pica
founts it is 1/12.[63]

These spaces were used both to introduce the necessary breaks between
words and also to fill out short lines to the width of the column.

Optimums

Writers on typography have defined the optimum word-space according to
two different criteria, one of which is absolute, the other relative, and
neither of which is complete enough to be taken as definitive. The first is
the unitary approach based on the division of space; as a fraction of the em
according to the divisions shown above. Dowding recommends as a norm
the 'thin space' of 1/5 of an em,[64] while Oliver Simon's 'rules of composition' state that 'Lower-case matter should be set with a thin or middle space
between words rather than a thick or wider'[65]

   The second approach is a relational one, based upon the width of key
letters in the chosen typeface. Tschichold's *Composition Rules* state that 'As
a rule, the spacing should be about a middle space or the thickness of an i in
the type size used',[66] while Martin recommends that it should be 'some-
where between width of the lower-case l and the n, and no greater than the

[63] Burnhill, *Type Spaces: In-house Norms in the Typography of Aldus Manutius*, p. 25

[64] Dowding, *Finer Points in the Spacing and Arrangement of Type*, p. 7

[65] O. Simon, *Introduction to Typography* (London: Pelican, 1954), p. 7

[66] C. W. de Jong, *Jan Tschichold: Master Typographer* (London: Thames and
Hudson, 2008), p. 274

width of the m'. He goes on to say: 'spacing is proportional to the design of the typeface . . . condensed faces and some italics, will require relatively smaller gaps between words than those with a generous set width'.[67] This approach has the merit of responding to variations in the style of the letter, taking into account the characteristics of the font, notably the width and the weight and consequent variations of interior space. The amount of space necessary to achieve a satisfactory division of words will depend not only upon the amount of letter spacing used within the words, but also upon the amount of space within the letters. Rosner says 'for faces of a narrow set . . . it is possible to use a thin space without causing difficulty in the separation of words'.[68] As we have seen in Chapter 2, fonts of a greater weight may also have smaller interior spaces requiring smaller intercharacter space and in turn correspondingly smaller word-spaces. Current technology has made it easier to apply these principles, and word-space can now be more readily adjusted to the characteristics of the font, either at source by the type designer, or by adjustments introduced by the typographer. Digital type design uses a division of the em-square into 1,000 units. A 250 unit space therefore equates to the metal 'four-space', and the 200 units space to the metal 'five space'. In contemporary digital typography, the word-space is an attribute of the typeface; a 'glyph' with a fixed width but no positive form. Rather than conforming to a single system of spaces as required by metal type, it has become a specifically designed component of the font; determined by the designer as part of the font design process and not – as some imagine – by the operating system or software programme.

3.4 Justified Type

Discussion of word-space so far has been based upon the uniform spacing that is a significant feature of ranged or 'flush-left' setting. This is compromised when the type is set 'justified'. In text that has been set ranged left, with a ragged right margin, a single optimal word-space can be established on the basis of the factors we have identified: the typeface design, the need to consolidate the word-unit, and the relationship to leading. This spacing

[67] Martin, *An Outline of Book Design*, pp. 39–40
[68] Rosner, *Type: Principles and Application*, p. 19

can then be applied consistently to the whole text. In lines of justified type however, word spacing is varied to achieve a consistent 'fit' to the column. Left unadjusted, the resulting increase in spacing can lead to 'rivers' in the texture of the print area; a visual impression of white lines flowing down the page linking successive word-spaces as vertical strips. To some extent the adjustments necessary to achieve the even right margin, will necessarily compromise those qualities of unity and consistency cited as the basis for ideal word spacing. Insensitive justification may result in too much word-space to maintain unity in the line, or too little to maintain the differentiation of words.

For much of the history of printing, justification has been achieved through variation in word spacing, augmented by hyphenation and, in early printing, the use of multiple variant sorts of differing widths. Mechanical composition by the Linotype system involved an ingenious mechanical process which was not limited to fixed intervals: the spaces between the words were regulated by use of spacebands; wedge-like dividers that could be moved up or down between the matrices to reduce or increase the space. This anticipates the more 'fluid' spacing later achieved by photosetting and then by digital media, which have also enabled greater flexibility by incorporating the spacing of letters as an additional tool for justification.

Justification by Letter-Spacing

The extent to which letter-spacing should be used to moderate the effects of variation in word-spacing will be a matter of individual judgement by the typographer. While it can enable us to better maintain the proportional relationship between word and letter space, it can compromise the visual unity of the word-unit or lead to visible variations in the weight and texture of lines within a paragraph. Different approaches to the relationship of these two variables involve either applying them in sequence or in conjunction. For the 'old-school' typographer whose frame of reference is informed by metal setting, word-spacing parameters would be established first and variations in letter-spacing would only be introduced after the possibilities of the first approach have been exhausted and variation of word-spacing has failed to provide a satisfactory result. The 'digital native', however, may make equal and interdependent use of word and letter-spacing together.

Line Measure

Justification is also closely affected by line measure: the number of characters per line, determined by type size and column width. Fewer words per line will in turn result in a smaller number of spaces, with the consequence that variations of word-space will be greater and more prominent. The shorter the line measure, the greater the risk of irregular variations of word-space.

Variation in word-space from one line to the next is not only an aesthetic problem but also a practical one. Even if the words are sufficiently separated, the semantic properties of the space as invisible symbol or 'silent letter' will be compromised if its proportions are not constant. Both this and the irregularity in the visual unity of the line will have an effect upon the reading experience, and it has been noted that dyslexic readers have greater difficulty with the irregular word-spacing of justified text than with the uniform word-space of text that is ranged left.

3.5 Conclusion

We have seen that the amount of space needed between words is governed by several considerations, some inter-related and some seemingly opposed. Word-space can be optimised according to an identifiable set of practical, material, and cultural factors, balancing the need to achieve a consistent visual reading of the word-space and the consequent visual 'word units' against the cultural norms of the justified page. These demonstrate a clear opposition between linguistic and formal concerns, and require the typographer to find an appropriate balance between them. To fulfil its intended function, the word-space needs only to be sufficiently greater than the letter space to avoid any confusion between the two, but narrow enough to maintain the visual unity of the line. Space between words is semantically necessary to distinguish them for the reader, while excessive word-space breaks the visual cohesion of the line, and the even visual rhythm of the text block. When set against the importance of a well-defined distinction between words, concern for unity of line might appear to be largely a matter of visual aesthetics, but when the action of the eye is considered in relation to the interlinear space, it becomes clear that excessive or irregular word-space may compromise the readability of the text as a whole. The ideal of an absolute optimum space contradicts the dominant concept of justification, which requires variability of word-space to fulfil the formal convention of an even right-hand margin. As Martin and Rosner confirm, the spatial characteristics of the typeface, and particularly the weight, 'set', and open-ness of the letters, will determine the optimum word spacing which will in turn inform decisions over the amount of leading, which we will consider in the next chapter. These are variables around which the skills of the typographer come into play, and writers on typography acknowledge the way that interdependent considerations of typeface style, word spacing, and leading inform professional judgement to determine the quality of the reading experience.

4 The Space between Lines

The relationships between letter-space and word-space lead us to a further visual feature interdependent with these: the space between lines. This chapter will trace the development of interlinear space as a variable independent of type size, considering its impact in different reading contexts and the connotative values that it can evoke. Interlinear space is described by the term 'leading', derived from the practice of inserting strips of type metal between the lines of metal sorts, to increase the space between the lines of print. This determines the visual density of the text on the page. It is therefore a key aspect of page layout and ease of reading, as confirmed by Dowding, who states that 'in a well composed page the white space is available for use *between* the lines where it serves the useful purpose of aiding readability'.[69] Leading can be moderated for reasons of page economy, to fit more lines of words onto a page or to 'pad out' a short text to a credible page count, or used to compensate for other features of the design such as unusually long line measures. Adjustments to leading can often improve readability more effectively than increases of size, and can therefore be a more efficient way of ensuring an optimum number of comfortably readable words to the page. The previous chapter has identified the need to ensure that the spaces between words are visibly smaller than the spaces between lines. In *Design with Type*, Carl Dair makes the point that 'where the space between the words exceeds the space between the lines ... the mass has a spotty, uneven texture'.[70] To avoid this and maintain the integrity of the word-shape requires a considered relationship between word-space and leading.

4.1 Origins: Leading and the Enlightenment

Burnhill quotes Mosley: 'Leading of text matter for aesthetic reasons is largely an eighteenth century (and later) habit'[71] and notes that founders in earlier centuries 'generally cast types to fit the body very tightly, and that

---

[69] Dowding, *Finer Points in the Spacing and Arrangement of Type*, p. 7

[70] C. Dair, *Design with Type* (Toronto: University of Toronto Press, 1995), p. 36

[71] Burnhill, *Type Spaces: In-house Norms in the Typography of Aldus Manutius*, p. 11

printers used them without leading', while Nash identifies Caleb Stower's 1808 *Printer's Grammar* as the first printed instance of 'leading' as a verb.[72] The development of leading as an independent variable in the design of a page aligns historically with the tendency toward rationalisation and reform in the work of Fournier and Baskerville, and the systematisation of previously localised and arcane trade knowledge. Allen Hutt talks of the cryptic trade of printing 'becoming conscious of itself'[73] in this period, which Robin Kinross defines in *Modern Typography* as a time when printing became typography.[74] The idea that line-spacing might be considered independently of the type size is therefore a product of the enlightenment and extends the range of measurable choices available to compositors; it develops alongside Fournier's initiatives to rationalise stems of measurement and type sizing, which led in turn to the point system. This systematisation enabled metal leading to be produced in point thicknesses, enabling the integrated use of a common system for the calculation of the revised depths of interlinear space, and this probably accounts for the continued use of this concept in digital typography. (Smiejers is nevertheless disdainful of the term, which he describes as 'a muddled hangover from metal technology'.[75]) It remains valuable because it allows us to consider type size and line-spacing independently while using the same unit of measurement. Though sometimes specified in the rather cumbersome form of 'additional leading', a more common and concise use combines the leading value with the body size of the letter to express the increment from baseline to baseline as a single equation by which 10 point type on a 14 point leading is concisely expressed as '10 on 14' or '10/14'. Systematic leading prompted greater standardisation of type body height, and had by the twentieth century become so much a norm that Tschichold could state that 'Typesetting without leading is a torture for the

---

[72] P. Nash, 'Scaleboard: The Material of Interlinear Spacing before 'Leading'. *Journal of the Printing Historical Society*. 25 (2016), p. 80

[73] A. Hutt, *Fournier: The Compleat Typographer* (London: Frederick Muller, 1972), p. 12

[74] Kinross, *Modern Typography*, p. 9 [75] Smeijers, *Counterpunch*, p. 17

reader'.[76] The amount of leading that text might require will vary according to several interdependent factors, including not only the size and design of the type but also the page layout, the line measure and further considerations of context, and so cannot be satisfactorily reduced to a single formula.

4.2 The Nature of Interlinear Space

Like the space between letters, the concept of interlinear space might at first appear to be a simple binary distinction of dark and light, but reveals complex ambiguities and variations. As the clear divisions we would expect to govern letter-spacing prove in practice to include irregular, 'permeable' spaces around open counters and apertures, so the visual space between lines is subject to several variables, notably the volume of space above and below the lower-case letter. In lines of capitals, the relationship between the line increment and the visual space is quite a stable one, in which the interlinear space forms a clean strip of white. In lowercase setting; however, ascenders and descenders break these clean horizontals, to create an irregular shape, the volume of which is determined not by the drop from the baseline to the tops of the capitals but by the height of the lower-case letters. This zone is another instance of a significant space that has both practical and connotative implications. Martin notes that the eye travels above the line, observing that 'the recognition characteristics of a typeface are concentrated in the upper part . . . the upper half of a line can still be made out easily when the lower part is covered up, but not conversely'.[77]

Leading and the Typeface

The volume of white space between lines is governed by two factors. One is controlled by the designer of the page layout: the insertion of additional leading between the lines of type. The other is inherent in the typeface design: the height of its lowercase letters relative to the capitals, known as the x-height. These two factors are closely interdependent; a typeface with a higher x-height will require more additional leading to provide the same volume of white space as seen in a typeface with a lower x-height.

---

[76] Tschichold, *The Form of the Book*, p. 65
[77] Martin, *An Outline of Book Design*, pp. 26–8

This varies significantly from one typeface to another; lower in types of the Venetian humanist style and higher in the neo-grotesques of the mid-twentieth century. Rosner explains the significance of x-height to space in these terms:

> Typefaces which possess long ascenders and descenders have comparatively small x-heights; consequently, when a number of lines of such type are set, they show a fair amount of white space between the lines, whereas typefaces which have large x-heights show less space between successive lines of type. Recognition of these facts is the basis of the best book typography.[78]

The ratio of x-height to capital height in types of different designs will therefore present differing volumes of interlinear visual space when set to the same leading. Dowding observes that 'Types of normal ex-height like Bembo, Centaur or Perpetua ... will look well ... with considerably less leading than will types of large x-height like Times Roman'.[79] He goes on to relate leading to the overall weight and stroke contrast of the typeface: 'faces which are light in colour like Monotype Baskerville, Caslon and 'Garamond' need less leading than do the more colourfully weighted faces like Times Book. In *The Elements of Typographic Style* Robert Bringhurst adds the concepts of axis and autography as factors, suggesting that:

> Large-bodied faces need more lead than smaller-bodied ones. Faces like Bauer Bodoni, with substantial colour and a rigid vertical axis, need much more lead than faces like Bembo, whose colour is light and whose axis is based on the writing hand.[80]

---

[78] Rosner, *Type: Principles and Application*, p. 11

[79] Dowding, *Finer Points in the Spacing and Arrangement of Type*, p. 12

[80] R. Bringhurst, *The Elements of Typographic Style* (Vancouver: Hartley and Marks, 1997), p. 37

The interlinear space is also interrupted by descenders, which vary in their depth and are generally deeper in 'book' faces designed or adopted specifically for long-text setting, where a low x-height and consequently pronounced ascenders aid the eye's recognition of word shapes. Tracy observes that 'for my own taste, if x to h is a proportion of about six to ten a face will look refined and be pleasant to read. If the x-height is much less than that the face may be stylish but will be unsuitable for long text. A larger x-height conduces to dullness'[81] and goes on to say that 'the accepted opinion now is that in a type designed for book printing the capitals should be shorter than the ascenders'.[82]

As a feature of type design, x-heights mark a distinction between tradition and modernity. The deep space of a letter with a low x-height is perceived as 'bookish' and inclines stylistically toward the historic traditions of the serif face, while higher x-heights are a key characteristic of the mid-twentieth-century neo-grotesques. The most celebrated of these, Miedinger and Hoffman's 1957 Helvetica, is distinguished from its late-nineteenth-century predecessor Akzidenz Grotesk primarily by its significantly higher x-height.

Leading and Line Measure

Decisions on leading are also interdependent with line measure; the number of characters to the line. It is widely recognised that lines of more than around ten words make it increasingly difficult for the eye to trace back and identify the beginning of the next line. Dowding identifies the need 'to ensure that the type and the measure are so related that the eye ... is not hindered in finding the beginning of the following line'.[83] This problem of line-identification is exacerbated by tight grouping of lines and ameliorated by more open leading.

Additional Line-Space

The introduction of additional interlinear space may also be used to signify a break or change in the text. While it has become a widespread convention

---

[81] Tracy, *Letters of Credit*, p. 51 [82] ibid.
[83] Dowding, *Finer Points in the Spacing and Arrangement of Type*, p. 9

of word-processing to put a line-space after every paragraph, this practice does not occur in book work, where it would be both visually intrusive and uneconomical. An additional line-space in a book page therefore normally signifies a greater change or distinction than would be indicated by a simple paragraph break. These breaks are normally of one line thickness or more for the practical reason of 'backing-up', maintaining an alignment with the leading intervals of the lines on the reverse of the page in order to minimise any intrusive 'show through'. Where the space indicates a separate body of text such as a quote, half-line-spaces may be used, on the principle that a half-line before and a half-line following will return the alignment to the consistent intervals of the baseline grid as discussed below. In both cases, the added line-space has a semantic function.

4.3 Book Typefaces and the Reading Experience

As we can see, leading influences the reading experience at several levels. It interacts with the word-spacing to delineate word-shapes, and distinguishes the line as a unit. It enables ease of reading over longer lines, providing a distinction between the lines enabling the eye to track back from the end of one line to the beginning of the next.

It also provides for connotative associations derived from the norms of long-text setting for books. It is generally accepted that the continuous text of books will require deeper leading than is necessary for the shorter texts of newspapers and ephemeral printing. As we have observed, book typography favours typefaces with well-defined ascenders and descenders, resulting in a generous interlinear space. This in turn provides for the use of typefaces with lower x-heights that aid the recognition of word-shapes. As the range of typographic options has become more diverse, and technological change has allowed for greater specificity of intended purpose, typefaces have come to be designed specifically for book work and the 'book face' has become an established genre with its own norms, as outlined in Chapter 1. Characterised by high ascenders and deep descenders, these typefaces are specifically designed for generous leading. The design of the face is therefore informed by ideas of the space in which it is to be used; type designed for the context of the book page anticipates the deeper leading that this entails.

These features have in turn developed more general associative connotations, and may be used to evoke an atmosphere of 'bookishness' in other contexts such as advertising or web design.

4.4 Leading and Value

Generous leading introduces 'breathing space' and carries important paratextual messages. It invites a slowing-down, and suggests to us that the text merits our careful and considered attention. It also prioritises a congenial reading experience and establishes a context in which the content of the words is valued over expediency or economy of production.

It is therefore a visible and readable indicator of the status of author or publisher. It marks the distinction between a cheap paperback produced with a view to getting the maximum number of words to the page, and a considered piece of fine printing which foregrounds the aesthetic dimension of the reading experience. Under the patronage of Duke Ferdinand of Parma, Giambattista Bodoni was given unusual scope to demonstrate extravagant standards of quality in printing and typefounding, in order to reflect the taste, refinement, and financial status of his patron. Both the margins and the leading of his books are generous, conveying the message that cost has not been an object; that paper can be used extravagantly, that economics have been less important than the display of wealth, status, and connoisseurship. William Morris's Kelmscott books offer a contrasting spatial aesthetic, which refers back to the typography of the Venetian typefounders. His own Golden Type in the 1892 edition of Ruskin's 'The Nature of Gothic' appears 'set solid' without additional leading; ascenders and descenders nearly touch, but the low x-height of the typeface compensates for this. The relatively open letter spacing combines with the tight leading to create a texture that echoes the surrounding ornamentation and engages the reader in a similarly immersive experience. This suggests to us that the text is to be directly apprehended, as a domain we enter and experience upon its own terms. Dense, thorny, richly patterned, his books were described by Meynell as 'grand to regard but difficult to read'.[84] Certainly the dense texts do not encourage ease or speed of reading, but

---

[84] F. Meynell, H. Simon (eds.), *Fleuron Anthology* (London: Ernest Benn, 1973), p. xi

when the book is considered as an artefact in the wider context of Morris's ideology, the very obstructiveness of the typography – the heavy types, the constraints of the leading, and the tendency to fill space with border and ornament – suggests the need to read slowly and carefully, to enter an environment removed from the urgencies of modern life. In both examples, the designer's decisions on the leading help to determine the reading experience.

4.5 Leading as Dialogic Space

The space between lines can also be read as a visual metaphor for the formation of meaning; we 'read between the lines' and this space gives shape to the arena in which interpretation and debate occur, recalling the rich traditions of interlinear sub-text and addenda that characterised manuscript culture long before the advent of the printed book.

The open interlinear space that emerges in the typography of the enlightenment suggests an invitation to analysis and interpretation, implying the scope for those secondary insights that occur 'between the lines'. While the manuscript page shows these as actual addenda, here their possibility is signalled as open to the reader, in a significant shift from a reading culture based in the authority of church and state to one based in reason and critical enquiry. The early printed book can be seen as an instrument for the documentation of absolutes: legal, religious or political, rather than prompting or engaging with a continuity of debate. By comparison, the interlinear space of the enlightenment page implies, and invites, interlinear thinking. From the 'modern' period onward, deep leading reflects the idea of pluralistic debate and indeed anticipates the idea that meaning is formed in the interpretation of the reader. In contrast, the close linespacing of the Kelmscott book does not suggest or invite critical debate or divergent readings.

4.6 Interlinear Space and Page Composition: Leading and the Grid

For the systematically minded designer, the intervals of the leading form a unitary 'building block' for the development of the page grid, a relationship we will consider in detail in Chapter 6. Bringhurst defines the leading as a 'basic rhythmical unit',[85] which in turn determines the baseline grid; an underlying pattern of lines at consistent vertical intervals which forms the skeletal structure of the page. In the carefully managed interaction between page margins and interlinear space, the text comes to 'inhabit' the page through a consistent pattern of fixed intervals. The lines of type form the 'weft' (or in American usage the 'woof') in the overall texture of print, to create a stable visual relationship between the words and the material substrate they occupy. Bringhurst writes, 'the typesetting device, whether it happens to be a computer or a composing stick, functions like a loom. And the typographer, like the scribe, normally aims to weave the text as evenly as possible',[86] while Dair uses a similar analogy: 'The line is to the mass what the threads are to the whole cloth.'[87]

4.7 Conclusion

The practice of leading emerges with the enlightenment, concurrent with a shift in attitudes to the formation and exchange of knowledge. It has become in turn one of the key variables to be manipulated by the typographic designer, in conjunction with decisions on typeface, word-spacing and line measure, each of which can influence the leading required. Leading has practical implications for the readability of the page, consolidating the autonomy of both the word-unit and the line-unit, and providing for the tracking of successive lines by the reader's eye. The resulting variations in the disposition of interlinear space can also signal stylistic tendencies and notions of added value. The fixed intervals of leading provide a unitary basis for the systematic page grid, central to the graphic vocabulary of modernism. Further, leading can symbolise a dialogic space, visually implying the idea of interlinear reading and interpretation. Leading is thus a practical tool, a cultural indicator, and a conceptual metaphor. As a unitary device it plays a significant role in the development of the modernist page, which will be considered in the next chapter.

---

[85] Bringhurst, *The Elements of Typographic Style*, p. 36 [86] ibid, p. 25
[87] Dair, *Design with Type*, p. 35

5 Space and the Margin

The previous chapter considered the implications of justified type for the space between letters; this chapter will address the role of justified and unjustified alignments for another area of significant space in which one of the defining dualities of twentieth-century design is enacted, introducing the opposing principles of symmetry and asymmetry and the cultural associations these evoke. The margin is more than simply unoccupied space on the page; it is the connective tissue of the designed document; a frame of uniform proportions. The relationship between the margin and the print area determines the integration of the printed text with the materiality of the book. Its significance is affirmed by Bringhurst: 'Perhaps fifty per cent of the character and integrity of a printed page lies in its letterforms. Much of the other fifty per cent resides in its margins.'[88] Stanley Morison described these qualities in terms of imposition or *mise en page* and said: 'Imposition is the most important element in typography – for no page, however well composed in detail, can be admired if the *mise en page* is careless or ill-considered.'[89]

It is in the margin that the qualities of negative space declare themselves most immediately to the reader, and the active values of 'empty' space may be observed. Martin states that 'the value of white space – designers in many fields refer to its "active" role – is a difficult concept for the layman to grasp.'[90] Dair expands upon the 'active' dimension of white space around the print area:

> the dominant characteristic of any mass is of course its shape; the area it defines against the white of the paper. Because typography is for the greater part limited to horizontal and vertical elements, mass will generally appear as a rectangle or a square.[91]

[88] Bringhurst, *The Elements of Typographic Style*, p. 165
[89] Morison, *First Principles of Typography*, p. 7
[90] Martin, *An Outline of Book Design*, p. 44 [91] Dair, *Design with Type*, p. 41

As with each of the aspects of space considered in previous chapters, decisions concerning the margin are interdependent with other factors, notably the line-space. Dowding observes that 'the relationship between the leading and the page margins must be watched for any increase in the former usually calls for more generous margination to offset it'.[92] For the justified textblock of the traditional book layout, the margin forms a frame; a concept we will return to in Chapter 8. The wider implications of this idea are evoked by Simon in his observation that 'Margins set off and enhance the type area, just as the mount of a drawing displays a picture to its fullest advantage'.[93] Like the dualities of form and counterform considered in previous chapters, the textblock and the margin of a well-designed page form interdependent parts of a whole. Writers on typography tend towards dynamic terms when describing this relationship: Bringhurst states that margins 'must lock the textblock to the page and lock the facing pages to each other through the force of their proportions',[94] while Dair asserts that 'marginal relationships should be unequal . . . and unequal relationships will create strong movements within the composition'.[95]

The proportions of the book margin have been analysed by Tschichold and others wishing to establish norms of visual harmony, and the study of manuscripts and incunabulae has revealed geometric principles that guided scribes and early printers in determining the relationship of text area to page. As with many such discoveries, the discovery of 'hidden knowledge' has often led commentators to confer on these working methods an occult status and indeed to infer that they embody wider universal truths or 'natural laws' (the postmodern graphic designer Jeffrey Keedy coined the term 'proportion voodoo'[96]). The 'canons' of J. A. van de Graaf, Villard de Honnecourt, Raul Rosarivo, and Jan Tschichold all make use of the same

[92] Dowding, *Finer Points in the Spacing and Arrangement of Type*, p. 11

[93] Simon, *Introduction to Typography*, p. 20

[94] Bringhurst, *The Elements of Typographic Style*, p. 165

[95] Dair, *Design with Type*, p. 111

[96] E. Lupton, *Deconstruction and Graphic Design: History Meets Theory* (2004). Retrieved 26 October 2022, from www.typotheque.com/articles/deconstruction_and_graphic_design_history_meets_theory

basic principle, using the points at which the diagonals of the single page cross with the diagonals of the page spread to determine the margins. In each case, the margin divisions are derived from the proportions of the page, creating a geometric relationship between the white rectangle of the page spread and the two vertical rectangles of the textblocks. These approaches create a deep space at the base of the page; a lower margin which might make sense in the context of a lectern bible, but will appear an unaccountable waste of paper to the publisher of a pocket-sized book. Richard Hendel notes that 'The large bottom margin is another of those conventions of ideal renaissance proportion that we now think of as rules. Explanations of why these margins have become standardised may only be rationalisations for what we have become used to seeing but that doesn't mean they can be ignored'.[97] In this, Hendel acknowledges the significance of user expectation.

Conversely, many examples of late-twentieth-century modernist book design are characterised by very shallow margins at top and bottom, while allowing for a much more generous play of space to the left and right.

5.1 Asymmetric Text and Gill's Ragged Margin

The relative merits of justified and ranged text can be viewed from several aspects. The impact of justification upon word spacing has been discussed in the previous chapter, while the following chapter will consider the wider implications of ranged setting in asymmetric column structures. This chapter will focus upon the visual qualities of the ragged margin resulting from the 'ranged' or flush-left text. Eric Gill's 1931 *Essay on Typography*[98] embodies a key debate of twentieth-century typography in proposing ranged-left text for book work, before the idea of asymmetric text was assimilated into European modernist design. It reveals a curious approach, in which a compulsion to form opinion seems to outpace practical understanding or reasoned argument. After setting out the case that uneven spacing is in itself objectionable and that uneven length of lines is not (while also stating that uneven length of line in a page of prose is 'not desirable'), he concludes that

---

[97] R. Hendel, *On Book Design* (London: Yale University Press, 1998), p. 35
[98] E. Gill, *An Essay on Typography* (London: Penguin, 2013)

'it is better to sacrifice actual equality of length rather than evenness of spacing'.[99] Most modernist typographers would agree with Gill on this point, but he then goes on to say that 'a measure of compromise is possible so that apparent evenness of spacing be obtained without unpleasant raggedness of the right-hand edge' and that 'without making his spacing visibly uneven' the compositor 'can so vary the spaces between words in different lines as to make the right-hand edge not unpleasantly uneven'.[100] The frankly implausible 'not visibly uneven' right-hand edge is one of many fault lines in this argument. It proposes that the supposed 'unpleasant' qualities of a ragged right margin might be a matter of degree, and that a reduced degree of raggedness would be correspondingly less 'unpleasant'. Most designers would argue that 'symmetric' and 'asymmetric' are absolute concepts, defined by their opposition to each other, and that 'reduced asymmetry' is not a working principle likely to produce design of any integrity. The irregular right edge of Gill's text in the *Essay* is neither ragged enough to make an assertive statement of asymmetric principle, nor straight enough to conform to traditional norms of symmetry. The 'slightly less ragged' appearance is also gained at the cost of many features that otherwise commend ranged text. Not only is the consistency of word spacing sacrificed as it is adjusted line by line, but the desired effect requires a high incidence of hyphenation (sometimes of words as short as five letters), and even the substitution of an ampersand for 'and' and the abbreviation of certain words (such as 'tho' on p 15) to achieve a better fit. These compromises recall the practices of early compositors or scribes, and may have seemed acceptable to Gill for this reason, but would be hard to apply without the kind of dialogue between author and compositor that was clearly required in preparing his *Essay on Typography* for print. The result is neither aesthetically satisfying nor methodologically consistent, offering neither the consistency of letter and word relationships to optimise the reading experience, nor the consistency of structure to provide a pleasing appearance. Though this approach fails on several levels, it is historically significant in revealing a conflict of ideologies and philosophical positions, between a kind of nascent modernism and a craft aesthetic fashioned from ideas of an imaginary past. Crucial to

[99] ibid. p. 89 [100] ibid. p. 90

this is the refusal to recognise that centuries of knowledge from the evolution of printing might be of use in resolving these contradictions. This seems characteristic of Gill's contempt for the trade knowledge of the printing industry. While it seems unlikely nearly a century later that the conventions of justified type will ever give way to ranged setting for book work, Gill's approach does not make a persuasive case and may indeed have helped to discredit the idea and limit further argument on the matter.

5.2 The Rag

A column of ranged text sets a maximum right-hand extent, and one might simply take this to mean that every word that fits within this boundary is included in the line, and every word that exceeds it must of necessity be moved to the next. In practice, however, this rather crude rule can be moderated by the manual 'ragging' of ranged type. The reasons for doing this may be visual or semantic. When a line of ranged type ends with a short subsidiary word such as 'to', 'at', 'an', the designer/compositor may opt to move this word down to the next line, or it may be felt that a bold and unmediated rag is itself visually intrusive.

The effective balancing of word-space in justified type will often require some use of hyphenation, and the options for the typographer can be expressed as a simple equation between the amount of hyphenation and the quality of word spacing; one is achieved at the expense of the other. Tschichold says, 'wide spaces should be strictly avoided... words may be freely broken whenever necessary to avoid wide spacing',[101] explicitly prioritising the quality of word-spacing over the disruption to the reading experience caused by breaking a word.

While justified setting may require the hyphenation of words to ensure balanced word-spacing, one of the advantages of ranged alignment is that it can enable the designer to dispense with hyphenation altogether. In practice it is customary to review the set text to identify any instances that require the manual introduction of hyphens (typically those created by words of unusual length). Richard Hunt confirms that opinions on hyphenation vary, and states that 'You may prefer to avoid hyphenation but it is better than the

---

[101] de Jong, *Jan Tschichold: Master Typographer*, p. 274

alternatives of a bad rag'.[102] Hyphenation in ranged setting is therefore discretionary, and will reflect individual preferences – a 'good' or 'bad' rag is a subjective judgement, and one which has a significant effect upon the visual quality of the right margin. On the one hand, a consistent modernist line would be to abandon hyphens and embrace the ragged margin as a dynamic aspect of the composition, supporting the 'active' role of space identified by Dair. Many advocates of asymmetric setting prefer an assertive rag to one that looks 'nibbled' by hyphens and other adjustments. Hunt observes that 'not everyone agrees with Gill about the correctness of a tight rag. Some designers prefer a more 'toothy' rag, with more variation between short and long lines'.[103]

5.3 The Indent

Alignment to the left margin provides for meaningful interruption in the form of the indent, a device universally adopted in western typesetting to signify the beginning of a new paragraph. This replaces the use of a specific glyph used in medieval manuscripts and early printing, which still survives as a typographer's mark, the pilcrow. It is therefore a particularly explicit instance of space taking on a semantic function previously fulfilled by a graphic sign. To inset the opening word of a paragraph to a consistently deeper measure than the margin provides a visual signal far more efficient than the line-spaces widely used in word-processing. The indent is a device with a defined and particular significance and therefore a key example within the visual lexicon of typographic space; it is a space that we 'read'. The depth of this interval is a matter determined by the designer, closely related to the interdependent factors of word-spacing and leading. The widely accepted principle that the indent should not be *less* than one em has in some cases been interpreted as an absolute maximum: Simon states categorically that 'The first line of a paragraph should not be indented more than one em',[104] but any survey of contemporary typography will show many exceptions to this 'rule'. An alternative is to base the depth of indent upon another order of typographic space: the leading. This has the

---

[102] R. Hunt, *Advanced Typography* (London: Bloomsbury, 2020), p. 193
[103] Ibid. p. 190 [104] Simon, *Introduction to Typography*, p. 7

aesthetic virtue of reinforcing the relational pattern of leading-intervals identified in the previous chapter. The depth of the indent is also related to the word-space, as it should be visually distinct and substantially greater in order to indicate that its meaning is quite different. Indent depth is also contingent on line length, and some designers favour a deeper indent for texts with a longer line measure than would be practical for narrow columns.

The indent has a further function in identifying bodies of quoted text or other secondary material by a 'maintained indent' applied to successive lines of the quote, distinguishing the indented section from the main authorial text. The resulting variation between the text margin and the indented margin is another component in the lexicon of typographic space.

Indents are also widely used to distinguish dialogue from narrative. Referring to the printing of plays, Simon recommends that the names of the different characters can be set at the beginning of a line, but in each case the text following should be indented.[105]

The terms 'hanging indent', 'exdent', or the more awkward 'outdent' are used to describe the practice of visually signalling the opening line by setting it outside the margin rather than inside.

5.4 Associative Values and Cultural Norms

The margin is a significant and 'active' space evoking a variety of associative values, some of which predate the printed page. Drucker notes that 'the space around text blocks creates the measured pace for reading while referencing the specific histories of book design'.[106] One of the characteristics of the manuscript was the accumulation of written observations and imagery through interlinear commentary and marginalia. Like a deep leading, the space of a generous margin may also suggest the argumentative engagement of the reader. Even if we do not write in the margins, this capability pervades the design; the space signifies scholarly value and visually anticipates marginal commentary. The margin also provides for secondary printed text; the use of 'shoulder notes' for this purpose can be dated back to early printing and the marginal notes of the hand-written manuscript.

[105] ibid. p. 44 [106] Drucker, 'Quantum Leap: Beyond Literal Materiality', p. 30

The amount of margin space marks the distinction between the cherishable and the ephemeral, between fine printing and the pulp paperback. Margin space also signifies luxury and connoisseur values. Whereas Aldus had developed in the early sixteenth century an economic page aesthetic based upon portability, some 300 years later Bodoni's books for the *Stamperia Reale* were characterised by their exceptionally generous margins, displaying space as signifier of wealth; the conspicuous and unmoderated consumption of paper and boundless expenditure of time and expertise. These books are not functional tools to be carried by the scholar, but status objects to furnish and enhance the patron's library. Like bibles in previous times, they are objects of reverence for the enlightenment sensibility, and their margins are a significant aspect of their authority.

5.5 Conclusion

As this chapter has demonstrated, the margin is a significant and communicative typographic space. The designer's choices regarding its depth and shape can align it to contrasting design ideologies and determine both practical and connotative aspects of the reader experience. We have seen how this framing space can demonstrate either the classical symmetry of the justified page or the 'active' properties of asymmetric composition, a duality that will be explored in detail in the next chapter. The conventions of the straight left margin provide for the semantic properties of the indent. The margin space is also an indicator of value, evoking both the suggested engagement of the reader and the 'value-added' qualities of a luxury product, distinguishing fine bookwork from ephemeral print.

6 Asymmetry and the Modernist Space

This chapter will consider the opposing concepts of symmetry and asymmetry introduced in Chapter 5, in the context of typographic history and the emergence of asymmetry in modernist design. The New Typography of the 1930s, heralded by the Bauhaus and consolidated into a working method by Jan Tschichold in *Die Neue Typographie*, involved a radical reappraisal of the organisation of typographic space. The primary defining concept of twentieth-century modernist typography was the doctrine of asymmetry. Kinross notes that 'the idea is associated especially with twentieth century modernism, which rejected the principle of centring (associated with the old classical order, and unresponsive to particular meanings—apart from the one big meaning of classical formality) in favour of asymmetrical configuration (denoting informality and able to articulate meanings within a whole)'.[107] Asymmetry has therefore both a connotative dimension and a practical one. Symmetry was associated with the past: the young Tschichold locates the New Typography within an idealised rejection of tradition, making an explicit link between axial symmetry and a redundant history. Of renaissance and baroque title pages he says, 'The central axis runs through the whole like an artificial, invisible backbone: its raison d'etre is today as pretentious as the tall white collars of Victorian gentlemen.'[108] Josef Muller-Brockman similarly identifies symmetric layout, or 'midline typography' as a product of the renaissance.[109] By comparison, asymmetric design is frequently described in dynamic terms; 'active' where symmetry is passive: Tschichold describes it as 'the rhythmic expression of functional design'.[110] Asymmetry is a description of relationships of space, and its emergence as a design doctrine identifies the asymmetric space with modernity and new design values. The dynamic interaction of positive and negative space

---

[107] R. Kinross (ed.), *Anthony Froshaug Typography and Texts* (London: Hyphen, 2000), p. 46

[108] Tschichold, *The New Typography*, p. 66

[109] J. Muller-Brockmann, *Grid Systems in Graphic Design* (Sulgen: Niggli, 1981), p. 20

[110] Tschichold, *The New Typography*, p. 68

provides a convenient metaphor for the modern condition, particularly when set against the 'classical' orthodoxies of symmetric layout.

6.1 Asymmetry: Precursors

A prescient and innovative example of asymmetric typography occurs in the work not of a designer or printer but a painter. In 1890 James Abbot McNeil Whistler published his pamphlet *The Gentle Art of Making Enemies*, typeset to his own very exacting specifications. Its title page is a unique example of a fully considered asymmetric layout. AJA Symons drew attention to its excellence in *An Unacknowledged Movement in Fine Printing*, published in 1930, but considered it alongside the work of Ricketts, Beardsley, and others. While it shares the cultural context of the aesthetic movement, the design of *The Gentle Art* is of a completely different stylistic order, and can be seen to anticipate developments that were to be codified in Tschichold's 'New Typography' some forty years later.

The well-documented influence of Japanese visual culture upon Whistler the painter provides some clues to the distinctive visual philosophy of Whistler the typographer. Notable for the organisation of compositional space in 'arrangements' determined by visual harmonics rather than the conventions of spatial illusion, he drew upon the visual codes of nineteenth-century Japanese art for the dynamic organisation of independent three-dimensional observations upon a two-dimensional surface, analogous to Kinross's description of asymmetry as 'able to articulate meanings within a whole'. Symons noted that 'Directly, at least, his lesson went no further; he left no universal formula to be altered and adapted wholesale'.[111] Symons was writing in 1930, just two years after the first publication of Tschichold's *Die Neue Typographie* (but some time before its translation into English), and his 'universal formula' may be an oblique reference to the emerging idea of a 'new typography'. Whistler had no plan to reform the typographic standards of publishing, or even to infer any widely applicable conclusions from his typographic work. By comparison, Tschichold was to attempt if

---

[111] A. J. A. Symons, 'An Unacknowledged Movement in Fine Printing'. In F. Meynell, H. Simon (eds.), *Fleuron Anthology* (London: Ernest Benn, 1973), p. 307

not a 'universal formula', then at least a practical synthesis designed to translate otherwise abstruse avant-garde ideas into workable standards for the printing trade.

Symons's essay is also concurrent with Eric Gill's *Essay on Typography*, considered in the previous chapter, which advocated asymmetry in the ranged setting of text. This predates the full emergence of asymmetry as a fundamental principle of modernist typography, and so perhaps misses the full significance of Whistler's innovations some forty years earlier, and the extent to which these prefigured practices which were to become central to mid-twentieth-century modernist design. Symons contrasts *The Gentle Art* with the visual extravagance of William Morris's Kelmscott productions, to say that Whistler 'showed that by taking care, by the exercise of taste and judgment, the ordinary materials of the printer could be made pleasing both to the eye and to the mind'.[112] This concern for 'the ordinary materials of the printer' was to be a characteristic of Tschichold's work. The wider significance of *The Gentle Art* as a proto-modernist artefact has seldom been acknowledged. It is very briefly mentioned in Jerome McGann's *Black Riders* regarding its influence upon the Bodley Head books,[113] while Matthieu Lommen accords it several pages of *The Book of Books*,[114] but both tend to view it sui generis as an eccentric 'outlier' rather than considering its wider significance both for asymmetric layout and for the visual text, a theme we will return to in Chapter 7.

6.2 Asymmetry as Ideology

The development of modernist typography follows an emerging conception of the designer as an independent creative thinker, as reflected in Morison's observation that typography became 'doctrinal' as soon as it was included in the design curriculum in the early twentieth century.[115] What had previously been a body of trade lore and craft knowledge with some localised variations of approach became codified into belief-systems which, as

---

[112] ibid.

[113] M. Lommen, *The Book of Books* (London: Thames and Hudson, 2012), pp. 266–9

[114] J. McGann, *Black Riders* (Princeton University Press, 1993), p. 78

[115] Morison, *First Principles of Typography*, p. 65

Morison noted, attached it for the first time to ideas outside typography; ideas that 'symbolised a new aspiration'. This aspiration had parallels in other disciplines: Hollis affirms that 'The ideological foundations which underlay the New Typography had their counterpart in the New Architecture',[116] while Tschichold made the corresponding observation that 'The old typography is much more closely related to the façade architecture of the Renaissance and its associated styles' and that 'typography and the new architecture share common ground'.[117] This 'common ground' is obviously spatial. Typography and architecture share a concern for the organisation of space, and of functions within that space. The developing agenda of twentieth-century modernism provides for rich analogies between the passage of ideas on the printed page and the passage of individuals through architectural environments. In both, the designed space is a facilitating medium of visual wayfinding and place-making. Organising the asymmetric structure of typographic space upon the page thus became a social responsibility analogous to town planning and urban regeneration. Tschichold's *Neue Typographie* frames typographic thinking within a kind of social manifesto: 'the liveliness of asymmetry is also an expression of our own movement and that of modern life. It is a symbol of the changing forms of life in general when asymmetrical movement in typography takes the place of symmetrical repose'.[118]

6.3 Background and Foreground

The interdependence of form and space is fundamental to asymmetric typography, which implicitly challenges conventions of 'foreground' and 'background'. Symmetry sets up a clear boundary between inside and outside, setting active text against passive space. By comparison, Josef Muller-Brockmann asserts that 'The new typography uses the background as an element of design which is on a par with the other elements'.[119] Tschichold makes the crucial point that 'in asymmetric design, the white background plays an active part in the design', while also making clear that

---

[116] R. Hollis, *Swiss Graphic Design* (London: Laurence King, 2006), p. 53

[117] ibid. p. 116 [118] Tschichold, *The New Typography*, p. 68

[119] Muller-Brockmann, *Grid Systems in Graphic Design*, p. 20

the concept of 'background' is a redundant one: 'The new typography uses the effectiveness of the former "background" quite deliberately and considers the blank white spaces on the paper as formal elements just as much as the areas of black type'[120].

This reappraisal of spatial relationships echoes equivalent developments in other disciplines. Bachelard rejects the interpretation of the binary opposition 'inside/outside' as equivalent to being/not being,[121] while twentieth-century abstract painting developed a wider discourse around notions of 'foreground and background', which will be explored further in Chapter 7.

The space in an asymmetric layout differs from the margins of the symmetrical text-block not only in its form but in its nature. Where centred and justified type creates a conformity that is internal and self-reflective, forcing the remaining space into redundancy, the negative space of an asymmetric page is a necessary correlative to the printed area; integral to the dynamic of its tension and resolution. Asymmetric typography is therefore not simply a different approach to the organisation of space, but a radical rethinking of its significance.

6.4 Asymmetric Text

While the doctrine of asymmetric layout was adopted in pre-war Europe, the justified setting of text was more resistant to innovation, and remains a largely unquestioned convention in book typography. It is hard to find an objective basis for this beyond the authority of tradition and the resulting user expectation. The straight right-hand margin has no practical value for the reader, while, as we have seen, the process of justification creates new problems of readability. Its persistence tends to be explained in terms of 'aesthetics', and may also reflect the moral authority implied in ideas of 'balance'. We are taught that balance is good; a synonym for reasoned argument and objectivity, while the idea of 'imbalance' can easily take on the moral baggage of 'inequality'. Kinross notes that 'The English word "justify" has legal and theological senses, before its specialised typographic

---

[120] Tschichold, *The New Typography*, p. 72
[121] Bachelard, *The Poetics of Space*, p. 212

one, ... to prove, to vindicate, to absolve'.[122] The visual symbolism of the symmetric layout is unrelated to its function. In a left-to-right writing system, left and right margins have little or no practical equivalence. A justified column may be visually symmetrical, but the right margin of the text block has a completely different purpose from the left, and as a consequence the margins of the justified page might even be described as 'functionally asymmetric'. In the evolution of the twentieth-century modernist page, the doctrine of asymmetry in page layout precedes by several decades the adoption of asymmetric unjustified text. Kinross describes this as 'one of the markers dividing pre-war and post-war modernism',[123] and it was only in the post-war years that the asymmetry of ranged text was widely adopted by a later generation of designers. Asymmetry thus enters the rule-book of modernist design in stages, from the outside to the inside, first in the arrangement of larger masses and much later in the alignment of lines and margins. It was advocated first in terms of abstract dynamics, inviting analogies with architecture in the kind of cross-disciplinary reference that so characterises the Bauhaus. Fundamental to these is the second defining feature of modernist typography: the grid.

6.5 The Grid

The practical and rhetorical dimensions of asymmetry are embodied in the concept of the grid, the term used to describe the division of the page and text-block by fixed vertical and horizontal intervals, determining the width of text columns and the positioning of all typographic elements on the page. The resulting uniformity of positioning and width, enables the visual interpretation of semantic values, the differentiation of different kinds of content, and the flexibility to arrange type and image according to semantic order while maintaining an overall visual consistency. The visual and rhetorical relationships of type are changed by its location within a space and the grid provides greater scope and flexibility for the visual expression of these relationships than a simple symmetric page. It allows for the development of a complex asymmetric form across the whole layout of

---

[122] R. Kinross, *Unjustified Texts* (London: Hyphen, 2002), p. 289
[123] ibid. pp. 292–3

the page spread, while maintaining a consistent underlying structure. It is in the development of an asymmetric layout upon a grid that the concept of interdependent positive and negative space reaches its fullest expression.

The Grid and Leading

It has already been noted that fixed intervals of leading provide a consistent 'weave' of horizontal typographic space, and this principle can provide a primary unit for then determining the width of columns, indents, margins, and gutters. The resulting correspondence between line intervals and other elements of the page creates a visual interconnectivity between all the different aspects of the layout. The logic of such an approach would have been more immediately evident to Froshaug, working with the material intervals of quads and leading, than to designers working with the more disembodied media of photosetting in the 1950s and 1960s. Professional digital design programmes have developed to support this underlying method through the concept of the background 'baseline grid' that can be re-set to correspond to the designer's chosen leading.

6.6 The Typography of Order

As the grid has become emblematic of twentieth-century modernism, its use has at times owed less to its semantic function than to the visual rhetoric of standardised form. In 1927 Moholy Nagy had advocated 'unequivocal clarity in all typographical compositions' and stated that 'Legibility-communication must never be impaired by an a priori aesthetics. Letters may never be forced into a preconceived framework, for instance a square'.[124] This ambition, however, co-existed in uneasy balance with the visual symbolism of formal order. This is particularly evident in the 'fielded' grid, in which horizontal divisions replicate the intervals of the vertical columns. The resulting pattern of square units has little practical or semantic value, but provides an arresting visual impression of 'order'. On the one hand therefore the grid provides for the rational and consistent organisation of multiple levels of information upon the page. On the other, the grid structure evokes

---

[124] L. Moholy-Nagy, 'The New Typography'. In M. Bierut, J. Helfand, S. Heller, R. Poynor (eds.), *Looking Closer 3* (New York: Allworth, 1999), p. 21

the ideals also attributed to mid-century modernist architecture, in which geometry serves a similar function as symbolic of social organisation, as ideological as Morris's rationale for revisiting the gothic and the medieval.

For post-war designers like Muller-Brockmann and his contemporaries the grid takes on philosophical and moral value. The rational organisation of space is presented as a social imperative; the page a kind of visual metaphor for the functioning of a well-ordered and productive society. By contrast, Douglas Martin's disingenuous observation that the grid is simply 'a cult word for a slightly more detailed margin scheme'[125] typifies the English 'new traditionalist' tendency. While this might be true of the simplest page structure, complex grids are considerably more than 'detailed margin schemes', particularly if they make use of multiple horizontal divisions and 'fields'. For the followers of the pre-war Tschichold they are emblematic; a logical extension of the doctrine of asymmetric typography.

Muller-Brockmann and the Grid

A key text is in the philosophy of the grid is Josef Muller-Brockmann's 1968 *Grid Systems in Graphic Design*. Introduced as a practical guide, it quickly reveals much wider ambitions and a distinct sense that we are dealing with a social and philosophical agenda. His reasoning typifies the modernist designer's approach to aesthetics – which is so say that it avoids discussion of aesthetics *per se* and substitutes the assumption that a suitably systematic analysis of function will of itself lead to an aesthetically satisfying outcome through 'the aesthetic quality of mathematical thinking'.[126] He states that 'anyone willing to take the necessary trouble will find that, with the aid of the grid system, he is better fitted to find a solution to his design problems which is functional, logical and also more aesthetically pleasing' and expands upon the social and moral dimensions of the concept: 'the use of the grid as an ordering system is the expression of a certain mental attitude inasmuch as it shows that the designer conceives his work in terms that are constructive and oriented to the future'. Within the first few pages

[125] Martin, *An Outline of Book Design*, pp. 45–6
[126] Muller-Brockmann, *Grid Systems in Graphic Design*, p. 9

Muller-Brockman has taken a method for the organisation of space and positioned it as an ideology, imbued with social value. The use of the grid system implies, he says, 'the will to systematise, to clarify; the will to penetrate to the essentials, to concentrate; the will to cultivate objectivity instead of subjectivity' and later the even more expansive ambition: 'The will to achieve architectural dominion over surface and space'.[127] By this point it is clear that rather than being informed about aspects of page layout, we are being initiated into a belief-system that is both comprehensive and exclusive. Throughout the book, practical instruction is interspersed with statements of moral value. 'the systematic presentation of facts, sequences of events, and of solutions to problems, should, for social and educational reasons, be a constructive contribution to the cultural state of society and an expression of our sense of responsibility'.[128] These may be rather lofty qualities to attribute to a system of margins and columns, but they are symptomatic of a period when the organisation of typographic space become an explicitly ideological matter.

Semantic Meaning vs Formal Order

While twentieth-century modernist typography might seem to present a fairly unified line of development, it reveals a fault line between two tendencies that have been identified by Kinross as the typography of semantic structure and the typography of formal order. In 'Typography Is a Grid' Froshaug takes the view that 'grid structures are implicit in the word typography',[129] viewing them not as an external construct but as an objective expression of semantic values, informed directly by the material properties of type.

This is a perspective readily available to a designer working with the material space of letterpress printing, a medium in which the margin and grid declare themselves in practice. The compositor's space differs from that of a calligrapher or lettercutter, or of the 'paste-up' of photoset text, in that it is not a surface onto which letters are to be placed, but a carefully

---

[127] ibid. p. 10   [128] ibid. p. 12
[129] A. Froshaug, 'Typography is a Grid'. In R. Kinross (ed.), *Anthony Froshaug Typography and Texts* (London: Hyphen, 2000), p. 187

constructed armature to hold them in position. As the medium within which type is held, the space has its own material structure.

Froshaug's perspective on the grid is based less in ideology than the material properties of type in the service of language. By comparison, in the work of some designers of the Swiss school the symbolic or ideological value of the grid seems to precede or override considerations of practical function or readability. The grid itself becomes a procrustean bed, dividing pages arbitrarily into square units, advancing abstract qualities over semantic ones. Muller-Brockmann makes the telling observation that 'the disadvantage of the 3 or 6-column layout is that the lines of text become relatively narrow and consequently a small typeface would need to be selected'.[130] Describing the problem in this way reveals that, in dramatic contrast to Froshaug's working principles or Moholy-Nagy's advice, Muller-Brockmann has constructed his grid first, after which he has considered the problems of fitting text into it. This strongly suggests that despite his claims to rational method, and notwithstanding the qualifier that 'this is a question that depends on the function to be performed', the sequence he proposes is one in which the grid division *precedes* decisions about type size. The grid then becomes a constraint to which text must be fitted, rather than being logically derived from decisions on face, size, and leading. The subsequent step-by-step instructions and indeed the layout of Muller-Brockmann's own book tend to support this view, and to suggest that the ideology, and the faith it invests in the pre-eminence of the grid, have become a precondition of the design rather than a practical tool.

Space as Abstract Form

Kinross notes that Froshaug was critical of Tschichold's diagrams of possible relations between elements in *Typographische Gestaltung*. 'The elements are abstract: as square, a circle, a line. Where is the text? The meaning? Reduced to pure form!'[131] Many of the first generation of the Swiss school were also visual artists (Gerstner and Lohse working as painters, Max Bill as sculptor and printmaker, among others), applying

---

[130] Muller-Brockmann, *Grid Systems in Graphic Design*, p. 57

[131] Kinross, *Anthony Froshaug Typography and Texts*, p. 38

through paintings and sculptures many of the same principles they developed in graphic communication. When formulating design principles as teachers and writers, they tended to approach the typographic space in abstract terms rather than linguistic ones, dealing in concerns of pure form rather than semantic structure, focusing upon spatial values and compositional dynamics more than relationships of language. This approach is characteristic of twentieth-century modernism and its promise of unified and comprehensive systems, by which generalisable knowledge can be systematically modelled. This pervades the doctrine of designer-teachers such as Armin Hoffman, expounding a formal language through largely abstract visual examples; innumerable square compositions in which positive and negative shapes are disposed in different ways to demonstrate variations of effect. In some instances these shapes are derived from letterforms, but typographic form is treated in the same manner as shapes drawn from other sources, some figurative, some wholly abstract. Hoffman's *Graphic Design Manual* begins with the dot and the line; signs and words enter later, in the abstract positioning of disembodied typographic elements, detached from any system of *inherent* space of the kind provided by the sidebearings of metal type or the fixed intervals of a baseline grid. Where Hoffman makes reference to grid structures it is to their abstract properties as systems of visual harmony and counterpoint, rather than their function in the organisation of content. The organisation of negative space serves to link these into an integrated whole, but the resulting space is more painterly than typographic.[132]

This rejection of traditional distinctions between image and language was typical of the time, but also reflects a twentieth-century notion of 'design' developed from the example of the Bauhaus, which assumes a broad equivalence between a wide range of production activities. Principles that link architecture, textile design, and product design can be applied only selectively to the design of written communication, and their application in this context brings a bias toward the formal and architectonic at the expense of the semantic. Designing products is different in

---

[132] A. Hoffman, *A Graphic Design Manual* (London: Academy Editions, 1988), pp. 50–64, 174–85

fundamental respects from the organisation of messages, and the assumption that these activities can share a common set of principles requires a very selective view of typography. These contradictions could only be reconciled by defining typographic 'fundamentals' in terms of abstract, formal properties, with a consequent bias towards the 'typography of order' over the 'typography of meaning and semantic disposition'. The resulting tension between formal and semantic values continues beyond the modernist era into the twenty-first century. Ellen Lupton notes in her essay '*Visual Syntax*': 'The dominant task of modern design theory has been to uncover the syntax of the language of vision, that is, ways to organize geometric and typographic elements in relation to such formal oppositions as orthogonal/ diagonal, static/dynamic, figure/ground, linear/planar and regular/ irregular.'[133] 'The language of vision' is a resonant and appealing phrase, but as Lupton's explanation confirms, this 'visual language' is quite distinct from the visual expression of language itself. The 'formal oppositions' described are abstract in nature. Grouping 'geometric and typographic elements' as interchangeable, or even subject to a common set of processes or decisions, risks reducing type to geometry and promotes its abstract qualities over its linguistic ones.

6.7 Legacies of Modernist Space

As we have seen, many examples of post-war modernist design merely imply ideas of clarity and order through their abstract properties, a 'typography of order' in which the order is primarily abstract, formal rather than linguistic. The grid structure and the corresponding values of negative space were a defining feature of post-war modernism of the Swiss school, which had by the 1970s become the dominant culture of the design establishment. Michael Bierut said of working for Massimo Vignelli in 1980: 'I had no doubt whatsoever that the purpose of graphic design was to improve the life of every person on earth beyond measure by exposing him or her to Helvetica on a three-column grid. That was certainty, and it made

---

[133] E. Lupton, 'Visual Syntax' in G. Swanson (ed.), *Graphic Design and Reading* (New York: Allworth, 2000), p. 73

design into a crusade.'[134] Swiss modernists had taken on key academic roles as arbiters of 'good' design and the orthodoxy of the grid had become the graphic voice of authority, providing in turn a symbolic target for the 'postmodern' graphic design of the 1990s.

One route out from these new conventions occurred not in the dominant technologies of photosetting and offset lithography, but in the letterpress workshop at the Künstgewerbeschule Basel in work by Wolfgang Weingart, explicitly concerned with relationships of space:

> I assigned my students exercises that not only addressed basic design relationships with type placement, size, and weight, but also encouraged them to critically analyse letterspacing to experiment with the limits of readability. We discovered that as increased space was inserted between letters, the words or word groups became graphic in expression, and that understanding the message was less dependent upon reading than we had supposed.[135]

Weingart is widely credited with creating a transitional bridge out of the increasingly sterile strictures of post-war modernism, through a personal idiom sometimes misleadingly called 'Swiss punk'. While his work shows a more disrupted and argumentative approach to semantic values, it continues to explore the dynamics of asymmetry and the visual dialectic of positive and negative space, through a relationship to the material processes of letterpress typesetting that he shares with Froshaug.

The subsequent period of 'postmodern' typography was characterised by designers' reluctance to settle on any single spatial method, preferring instead to set divergent compositional approaches in deliberate opposition. As the work that emerged from Cal Arts, Cranbrook and other centres

[134] M. Bierut, *Graphic design and the New Certainties* (2003). Retrieved 25 October 2022, from https://designobserver.com/feature/graphic-design-and-the-new-certainties/1617

[135] W. Weingart, *Elements in a New Context*. Retrieved 25 October 2022, from www.neugraphic.com/weingart/weingart-text3.html

diffused into to the mainstream through publications like David Carson's *Raygun*, the rejection of grid structure was a characteristic of the zeitgeist of the 1980s and 1990s. The term 'deconstruction' was enthusiastically if inaccurately co-opted to describe layouts that were deliberately fragmented, contradictory, and unresolved. It is debatable how far these experiments reflected an informed understanding of postmodern theory, but the term provided a vocabulary and validation for rebuilding graphic design, or at least for proposing more pluralistic approaches to design philosophy.

Once it has been identified with a dominant design culture, the very concept of a 'grid' can readily be identified as counterintuitive and constraining; the visual embodiment of a prescriptive orthodoxy. Rick Poynor's definitive study of postmodern graphics was entitled *No More Rules*, and the postmodern typographic space is a fractured, ambivalent, and self-conscious one. Symmetry is re-embraced for ironic or argumentative effect, often juxtaposed with asymmetry, in typography that is explicitly transgressive. The designer and artist Ed Fella adopted a systematic 'deconstruction' of typographic rule-making, developing a graphic language based upon very deliberate inconsistency. As well as the wilfully eccentric letterforms that populate his early designs, the space between and around the letters obeys only one underlying principle – that of variability. After this convulsive interval, the spatial properties of the modernist page-space have by now been so thoroughly absorbed into the mainstream that they no longer carry the ideological values they originally represented, reduced in most cases to a matter of stylistic choice rather than philosophical position.

6.8 Conclusion

Through the twentieth century, asymmetric space has been associated with modernity and the supposed rationality of a machine age. Modernist typographers rejected justification as an archaism, but justified columns persist within many otherwise stringently modernist page layouts through the 1950s. The pre-war modernism of the New Typography is concerned therefore more with the asymmetric arrangement of shapes than the asymmetric arrangement of text. This reflects a tendency for modernist typographers to view the page as an abstract composition of rectangular masses, and to adopt the resulting asymmetric geometry as visual metaphor for reason and order.

From this point we can trace an underlying divergence between two different approaches to the asymmetric space: as a field for the play of abstract values symbolising formal order, or a means to articulating the organisation of content. Originally a radical departure from the symmetric norms of the centred page of justified text, by the post-war years its doctrines of order and functionality had been embraced by a massified corporate culture to become, over time, a new orthodoxy. Where through history the order of the symmetric printed page had first signalled the authority of church and state, then of science and reason, the ranged type and grid structures of the Swiss school came to signify the authority of public services, then of multinational industries and corporations. In turn, the radical graphics of the 1990s represent many strategies for the rejection of these norms, in a body of work conveniently, if rather casually, characterised as 'postmodern'.

7 Typographic Space and the Visual Text

This chapter will consider the ways in which conceptions of typographic space have been central to the development of the 'visual text'. The interaction of typographic and pictorial values was a key characteristic of the twentieth-century avant-garde, through the converging preoccupations of writers increasingly concerned with the graphic form of the text and visual artists introducing written language into the pictorial space. Rather than attempt to deal separately with writing and visual practice, this chapter will therefore consider them as a whole, in order to trace the development of typographic space as a medium of creative experimentation.

In 1969 the Belgian artist Marcel Broodthaers produced a visual tran-scription of Stéphane Mallarmé's 1897 poem *Un coup de dés jamais n'abolira le hasard*, in which the lines of words are replaced by solid monochrome bars of the original type size. Only the spatial composition remains, indicating their position and density while withholding their verbal mean-ing, and isolating their compositional values from their semantic ones. Broodthaers states that 'Mallarmé is at the source of modern art ... He unwittingly invented modern space'.[136] This radical observation explicitly locates the basis for the visual innovations of the succeeding century in a poet's articulation of typographic space.

It is the nature of the avant-garde to question the authority of systems, and over the past 100 years the systems of language and visual representa-tion have frequently been juxtaposed to disrupt or critique each other. The incorporation of written language into visual art and the use of graphic form in poetry have been used to challenge and interrogate conventions of typographic and pictorial space. This has redefined the scope of each, and developed the relationships between them. The introduction of typographic space into the image, through bringing words into pictures, visually cri-tiques the illusionistic conventions of painting, while the manipulation of typographic space within the poem critiques the structural conventions of writing. Froshaug applies the concept of 'reading' to both, observing that

[136] R. Krauss, *A Voyage on the North Sea: Art in the Age of the Post-modern Condition* (London: Thames and Hudson, 1999), pp. 50–1

'poems and paintings have to be read to be understood: but whereas reading poetry is a sequential process ... reading painting is not'[137] and identifies the 'point of attraction and departure' for the eye as being determined by the painter.

7.1 Typographic Space in Poetry

The typesetting of poetry sets exacting responsibilities for the designer, as a field in which the disposition of space carries more complex significance than in the setting of prose. It involves unique practical constraints (book designers will agree that lines of a poem should not break unless broken by the author), but the typographic design of a poem is concerned with more than the practical considerations of readability or the abstract aesthetics of composition. Oliver Simon observes that 'the shape of a poem is not only pleasing to the eye, but is a help to the mind in grasping the rhythmic character of the poem. This is important in much contemporary poetry where no traditional metric scheme is followed'.[138] Dowding makes the interesting point that 'poetry is more concentrated than prose, and therefore has to be absorbed more slowly',[139] implying a visual 'reading' as well as a sematic one. The typographic setting of poetry makes explicit use of space as content. It articulates the space between words in not only material but also performative terms, indicating the pauses and breathings that determine a spoken rhythm.

We have already considered typographic space as a measure of silence, and relationships of sound and intervals of silence provide the defining constraints of many modes of poetry. From sonnets to haiku, poets have tested their ideas against the formal conventions of fixed numbers of lines and syllables, of rhythm and rhyming structure. Typography is similarly governed by meaningful constraints; working within limits of number and space, applying a consistent understanding within limitations of type-size, space, alignment, and leading, all with the aim of providing visual coherence.

---

[137] A. Froshaug, 'Between Poetry and Painting'. In R. Kinross (ed.), *Anthony Froshaug Typography and Texts* (London: Hyphen, 2000), p. 183

[138] O. Simon, *Introduction to Typography*, p. 48

[139] Dowding, *Finer Points in the Spacing and Arrangement of Type*, p. 8

These observations apply to the conventions of the printed poem; conventions that were to be repeatedly challenged or disrupted by experimental writing. The disruption of the typographic space for expressive or interrogatory purpose is a recurrent characteristic within twentieth-century poetry; a period in which we see the development of a 'visual poetics' or a poetics of typographic space.

Before Broodthaers' sintervention, Mallarmé's *Coup de dés* was itself revolutionary in presenting the act of writing as a process of visual design. Mallarmé differentiates the words and lines of the poem by typeface, size, italicisation, capitalising, and position: the words are scattered (or 'constellated') across the page.

This approach challenges the conventions of linear reading, instead engaging the reader in the act of constructing the poem from a variety of different points. This is analogous to the 'reading' that the viewer brings to the spatial codes of a painting, assembling meanings from the visual relationship of parts rather than from a linear sequence. Mallarmé's notes on the printer's proofs show very specific and measured decisions on the spatial composition of the poem. Bachelard observes that the geometry of inside-outside 'conveys spatiality on thought',[140] and this principle is explored and tested across Mallarmé's page-spreads. The *Coup de dés* engages with the interior space of the poem, embodying a concept later developed by dom Sylvester Houédard in defining concrete poetry as 'aware of graphic space as its structural agent'. He then says: 'A printed concrete poem is ambiguously both typographic-poetry and poetic typography – not just a poem in this layout, but a poem that is its own type arrangement.'[141] In this genre, the visual form of space is integral to the poem's development. It is clear that visual decisions determined and informed the writing of the *Coup de dés*, rather than simply 'framing' it. Mallarmé's work therefore instigates a practice of writing *with*, and *within*, typographic space; demonstrating the active use of space as medium. This in turn sets the scene for developments in twentieth-century modernist writing

[140] Bachelard, *The Poetics of Space*, p. 212

[141] D. S. Houédard, 'Pure Concrete'. In N. Simpson (ed.), *Notes from the Cosmic Typewriter* (London: Occasional Papers, 2012), p. 160

in the period between the First and Second World Wars, of which the poet William Carlos Williams said: 'It was when the whole world was going crazy about typographic form.'[142] Later examples include the semantic poetry of Stefan Themerson, which Kinross describes as 'an attempt to strip language down, and at the same time to embody– or body forth–meaning: typographically'.[143]

Not all of the canonical landmarks of avant-garde typography engage with typographic space, or could be strictly defined as typographic. Froshaug observes that 'Marinetti indeed made blasts toward the bourgeoisie, but could not give a guideline to writers or compositors'.[144] The *calligrammes* of Guillaume Apollinaire are significant in the evolution of visual poetry, but their relevance to this study is circumscribed by the way the typographic space they create and occupy departs so fully from the horizontals and verticals of print as to become largely pictorial. In those that use printers' type rather than handwriting, words and letters are arranged freely without any standardising of intervals. Conceived through a process of drawing, many continue the historic tradition of the 'figured poem', as figurative silhouettes or emblems.

7.2 Poetry and Printing

Johanna Drucker has noted that hand-setting type

> quickly brings into focus the physical, tangible aspects of language – the size and weight of the letters in a literal sense – emphasizing the material specificity of the printing medium. The printer controls not only the sequence of words and lines, but the shape of the surrounding space. The printer is an active participant in the making of meaning, and this becomes particularly significant in collaborations between writer and printer, or practices that integrate the two.[145]

[142] McGann, *Black Riders*, p. 43 [143] Kinross, *Unjustified Texts*, p. 298

[144] A. Froshaug, 'Pioneers of Modern Typography'. In R. Kinross (ed.), *Anthony Froshaug Typography and Texts* (London: Hyphen, 2000), p. 202

[145] J. Drucker, *Letterpress Language: Typography as a Medium for the Visual Representation of Language* (Cambridge: MIT, 1984)

As hand-set letterpress was superseded by machine composition, it joined other redundant technologies in gaining a new status as a 'craft': one which allowed the author more direct and interactive engagement with the printed word. Hope Mirrlees's 1919 poem *Paris*, one of the most typographically ambitious publications of Leonard and Virginia Woolf's Hogarth Press, explores typographic spaces and intervals in ways that would have been exceptionally difficult to achieve within the conditions of the printing trade, but were enabled by a publishing environment in which writers and publishers themselves took on the role of compositor.

Later, post-war writer-turned-printer Anais Nin observed: 'You are related bodily to a solid block of metal letters, to the weight of the trays, to the adroitness of spacing'.[146] Like Froshaug, she notes the significance of the printing process as a problem-solving medium.

The Typewriter

The increasingly direct engagement of writers with the visual form of their work was also prompted by changes in their writing tools. By the early twentieth century an increasing number of poets were writing on typewriters rather than in longhand, and the 'mechanisation' of writing provides the writer with a much more direct correlation to the regulated spacing of set type. In his study of typewriter art, Barrie Tullett defines the typewriter as a form of printing press.[147] Though typewritten letters are applied consecutively rather than simultaneously, they fulfil Smeijers's criterion for type since the spaces between the letters are predetermined by the mechanical properties of the machine, which require that all the letters are set upon bodies of identical width. The fixed spacing intervals of the typewriter therefore echoed the defining constraints of typesetting and enabled more specific instruction to the compositor regarding the spatial layout of the poem, narrowing the margin of interpretation between a manuscript and the printed outcome.

---

[146] A. Nin, *The Diary of Anaïs Nin 1939–1944*, Vol. 3 (Boston: Mariner, 1971)

[147] B. Tullett, *Typewriter Art: A Modern Anthology* (London: Laurence King, 2014), p. 15

The medium enabled the manipulation of typographic space by type-writer artists or visual poets including Houédard, Henri Chopin, and Bob Cobbing, and included interventions such as moving the paper while still on the cylindrical platen. The move from a manual, autographic writing medium to a mechanical one also marks a characteristic shift in modernist poetics; away from the continuity of the authorial voice, to the introduction of found or re-contextualised material to form a collage or *bricolage* of found words and phrases. This has a close parallel in early modernist painting, in which the introduction of typographic content into collages and cityscapes disrupts spatial conventions.

7.3 Painted Words: Typographic Space in Twentieth-Century Visual Art

To introduce letters and words into a representational space is a disruptive and subversive act; one that serves to expose fundamental artifices in the relationship between visual and linguistic systems. In *A Natural History of Typography* Ellen Lupton and J. Abbot Miller note the ambiguities of this relationship, and its significance for Saussure and the development of semiology.[148] Placing two-dimensional letters and words inside a pictorial space exposes the illusionistic compact of representation, and sets the two forms of space in a dynamic or argumentative opposition. The use of printed paper in the cubist collages of Picasso and Braque is inherently provocative, testing the boundaries of representation and visual experience while also introducing the contrary activity of reading into the framed space of visual art. Type and lettering were emblematic of the urban experience of the machine age, and the work of Robert Delaunay and Fernand Léger reflects the ubiquity of typographic forms in the twentieth-century cityscape, a tendency developed by the American precisionists in the period between the First and Second World Wars. Few of these examples are themselves strictly typographic in their spatial structure; what they share is

---

[148] E. Lupton, J. A. Miller, 'A Natural History of Typography'. In M. Bierut, W. Drenttel, S. Heller, D. K. Holland (eds.), *Looking Closer: Critical Writings on Graphic Design* (New York: Allworth, 1994), p. 21

the *representation* of typographic space and the disruptive introduction of this idea into the pictorial space.

Against Language: Space, Sound, and Orality

A distrust of the linear constraints of language has been a recurring theme of the twentieth-century avant-garde, and manipulation of typographic space has been used to articulate oppositions between 'linear' and 'spatial' thinking. Disruptive strategies such as the 'cut-ups' of William Burroughs borrow from visual practices which interrogate the authority of printed language. Since Mallarmé it has been possible to interpret the poem not simply as a linguistic document but as a sonic diagram, giving visual form to frequency and duration of sounds and silences; a representation of a performed work, or an evocation of how performance might occur, that is also a graphic entity in its own right. Under such circumstances the concept of 'reading' is extended beyond the limits of language into the visual specification and documentation of performance. Kurt Schwitters's *Ursonate* anticipates later avant-garde performance works, as a 'sound map' in which typographic space provides detailed measurements of silence as well as the vowels and consonants of his wordless vocalisations.[149] In this it draws more upon Schwitters's proficiency as a modernist typographer than the collages for which he is better known.

Subversion of Typographic Norms

The norms of justified type have also been subverted for creative effect. In concrete poetry and experimental typography, many of the unintended effects that printers aimed to minimise have instead been developed as deliberate features that highlight the role of space as 'structural agent'. In Bob Cobbing's *This Is a Square Poem* the exaggerated spacing by which the lines are justified to form a perfect square is foregrounded as a visual feature: the mechanism is made manifest in the poem's visual form.[150]

---

[149] K. Schwitters, *Ursonate* (1932). Retrieved 24 December 2022, from https://web .archive.org/web/20060216143920/http://ubu.clc.wvu.edu/historical/schwit ters/ursonate.html

[150] B. Cobbing, *Square Poem* (1932). Retrieved 24 December 2022, from https:// gammm.org/2022/06/18/square-poem-bob-cobbing-1989/

In Richard Eckersley's design for Avital Ronell's *The Telephone Book* narrow columns are justified to create intrusive patterns of space between words that align to the left and right margins.[151] In Tom Phillips's treated book-work *A Humument*, these 'rivers' are highlighted to become a graphic feature in their own right, connecting selected groups of words to present new meanings and counter-narratives from a treated text that has otherwise been obscured by his own graphic interventions[152].

Space and Abstraction, Mass and Field

Typographic design and visual art in the twentieth century show a common concern for the re-evaluation of positive and negative space. The relationship between mass and field has been a recurring preoccupation of abstract painting, and this closely parallels the revised significance of negative space in the New Typography as formulated by Tschichold. The significant void was an important concept in mid-century modernist sculpture, notably the work of Henry Moore and Barbara Hepworth. Jeanette Winterson says of Hepworth: 'Her version of "truth to the materials" means that space is as much a part of a Hepworth sculpture as mass.'[153] Through the century, painterly conventions of foreground and background, and fixed distinctions between mass and space, gave way to a more argumentative dialogue between these concepts, and the materiality of the field was a defining preoccupation in the movements described as 'colour field painting' and 'post-painterly abstraction'. In a 1998 interview the abstract painter Patrick Heron criticises 'collections of single forms against a "background" which is actually a vacuity' and contrasts this with Cezanne's painting, in which 'every part is equally solid and in the same instant equally spacious. Cezanne's space is *solid*'.[154]

The space in asymmetric typesetting is equally 'solid'; both in the sense that it originates in the material forms of quads, leading, and reglets, and

[151] A. Ronell, R. Eckersley, *The Telephone Book: Technology, Schizophrenia, Electric Speech* (Lincoln: University of Nebraska Press, 1991)

[152] T. Phillips, *A Humument*, 4th ed. (London: Thames and Hudson, 2005)

[153] J. Winterson, *The hole of life* (2003). Retrieved 25 October 2022, from https://www.tate.org.uk/art/artists/dame-barbara-hepworth-1274/hole-life

[154] M. Gayford, D. Sylvester, *Patrick Heron* (London: Tate, 1998), p. 38

that the design of this space has been planned and constructed. It collapses the distinctions between 'form' and 'ground' through an integrated design of positive and negative space. Where the symmetrical structure of a 'classical' eighteenth-century title page differentiates typographic foreground from margin background, Tschichold's early layouts present a dynamic organisation of space that develops the possibilities proposed by Whistler in *The Gentle Art*.

Heron's critique of inner and outer as foreground-background can also be applied to the interior space of letters. Discussing his 1964 painting *Purple Shape in Blue*, he describes the formation of the shapes as 'recessive' and says, 'Actually I did not "design" or "draw" or even consciously premeditate the shape ... What happened was that I allowed the blue ground to slowly eat into the purple area (from the outside).'[155] The idea of 'ground eating into area' is a subtractive process, like the removal of steel from the punch by which the printed letter was originally formed. Bachelard's rejection of the interpretation of the binary opposition of inside/outside as 'no longer to be taken in their simple reciprocity[156] corresponds to Heron's rejection of the binary distinction of object/space, and the wider discourse around the notion of 'foreground/background'.

7.4 Typography and Systems of Compositional Space

Lommen observes that the asymmetric layout of Whistler's *The Gentle Art* 'betrays his Japonisme'.[157] More than a stylistic tendency, however, it reveals a distinct and uniquely pluralistic approach to both typographic and representational space which anticipates some key developments in twentieth century visual art. Japanese methods of projection offer a flexibility of structure and spatial organisation that corresponds to the qualities Kinross attributes to asymmetric typography: 'able to articulate meanings within a whole'. In the assimilation of western influences into

---

[155] P. Heron, 'Purple Shape in Blue' in *The Tate Gallery Report 1964–1965* (1966). Retrieved 25 October 2022, from www.tate.org.uk/art/artworks/heron-purple-shape-in-blue-1964-t00711

[156] Bachelard, *The Poetics of Space*, p. 216

[157] Lommen, *The Book of Books*, p. 266

Chinese traditions, Japanese woodcut artists of the nineteenth century had arrived at a synthesis which was pluralistic and flexible, enabling differing ideas of three-dimensional depth to be selectively applied and combined. This offers an alternative to the systematic perspectives that had dominated western painting since the Renaissance, much as the ideal of axial symmetry had dominated the typographic layout of the book page. A further effect of the developing Japanese tradition was to 'tilt' the picture plane forwards, so that the horizontal planes faced the viewer as a two-dimensional surface, an oblique projection more analogous to a page of text.

More than an aesthetic preference, the influence of Japanese prints upon Whistler, van Gogh, and their contemporaries involved a profound re-figuring of accepted codes of spatial representation, anticipating the later developments of cubism. The compositional values that Whistler applied to the typography of *The Gentle Art* correspond those used in the paintings he defined as 'arrangements': finely judged compositions of rectangular elements, often largely monochrome, as in the *Arrangement in grey and black* popularly known as *Whistler's Mother*. Like the asymmetric grid, this approach allows visual information to be organised and structured according to relationships of content rather than conforming to an abstract convention such as a central axis or a vanishing point.

Whistler's typography also provides one link to twentieth-century visual poetics that remains unexplored. In 1887 Whistler became friends with Mallarmé, who translated Whistler's essay on art and aesthetics, *The Ten O'Clock Lecture*, in 1888. Whistler worked with Mallarmé on the design of various books, and in view of this continued association it can be assumed that the typography and production of *The Gentle Art* in 1890 had some influence upon the graphic development of the *Coup de dés* in 1897.

7.5 Conclusion

Comparison of two key figures in the complex history of the visual text reveals a significant distinction: if Apollinaire was drawing with letters, Mallarmé was writing with space. This interpenetration of disciplines is a characteristic twentieth-century phenomenon. It encompasses the 'free word', and the wordless typography of letter-clusters. It is defined, as

Houédard says, by 'space as structural agent': a term which extends beyond the confines of 'concrete poetry' to encompass and reference a wide range of other practices, and demonstrates Bachelard's observation concerning the 'spatiality of thought'. This quality is demonstrated in the synthesis of projection and perspective found in nineteenth-century Japanese art, which was to influence the use of asymmetry in Whistler's typographic layout.

These examples show how the visual text involves a 'reading' process that is compositional but not 'abstract', and alludes to the action and behaviour of language through a metalinguistic reading of typographic space, as a visual language that reflects upon the text.

8 Typographic Space as a Metalanguage

The preceding chapters have established that typographic space has the capacity to communicate values and ideas, as well as mediating content and organising the structure of information. From Burnhill's observations on the space added by renaissance publishers to denote topics for discussion, to the present-day conventions of the indent and the line-space, the use of typographic space enables the designer to clarify and delineate the relationships between the parts of a text, in a form that is then visually interpretable by the reader. Drucker notes that conventions for the organisation of text are themselves a set of codes that direct our reading, and the distribution and arrangement of verbal materials an integral part of the semantic value of any text.[158] As well as establishing differentiation and hierarchy, the disposition of space may align the text with the values associated with different design ideologies, or evoke ideas of material value. Sally Maier's 2015 master's thesis 'Design Dissection'[159] explores the concept of 'White space as a luxury good' and establishes a correlation between the percentage of white space used in publications, and the median household income of their readership. The use of space in the modernist grid signals a regard for design values and a notion of 'modernity' that has now become historically established. Sue Walker makes the point that 'the graphic presentation of written language can have a considerable effect on how it is read, interpreted and understood by readers'.[160] The wide margins and generous leading of a high-quality book page indicate that we will read carefully and reflectively; the tight leading and narrow margins and gutters of a tabloid newspaper reflect its ephemeral nature. Many of the traditional conventions of the page date from times when reading books was a high-status activity, and their continued use now differentiates books produced for the 'serious' reader, from the wider output of the popular press.

---

[158] Drucker, 'Quantum Leap: Beyond Literal Materiality', p. 28

[159] S. Maier *Design Dissection* (2015). Retrieved 25 October 2022 from http:// thesis2015.micadesign.org/sally/

[160] S. Walker, *Typography and Language in Everyday Life* (Harlow: Pearson, 2001), p. 172

Typographic space therefore has both micro and macro dimensions, which have been considered in preceding chapters, ranging from specific functional attributes to aspects of connotation and cultural value, notably the dialogic possibilities and economic signals embodied in interlinear and marginal space. Recognising these attributes as consistent and generalisable enables us to consider the idea of typographic space as a language.

8.1 Language: Definitions and Parameters

Language has been defined according to various criteria but could be summarised as a shared system of symbols by which members of a social culture express themselves. These may be spoken, manually signed, or written. The actual meaning of the term 'language' has also become a contested field in the light of postmodern theory, which views it as a semantically self-contained or self-referential system in which words do not represent static meanings but exist in a range of contrasts, in relation to the meanings of other words. The term is also applied with varying degrees of precision in different contexts, sometimes more as metaphor or analogy (this would include such popular terms as 'body language'). We have considered in Chapter 6 the concept of 'visual language', now used widely and uncritically across the visual arts, sometimes to denote no more than a personal idiom or style (a more accurate term for this might be a 'visual idiolect'). More broadly, as discussed in Chapter 6, it has been characteristic of twentieth-century modernist design to formalise systems of line shape and colour. In her essay *Writing Lessons: Modern Design Theory* Lupton notes that this abstract 'language' has been theorised as analogous to, but separate from, verbal language; and that modernist theories of 'visual language' compare verbal and visual expression in order to keep the two systems apart from one another.[161] She critiques this concept, with a view to 'finding a place within those assumptions for a more expansive "language of vision," one that intersects with verbal language rather than standing as its opposite'.

---

[161] E. Lupton, *Writing Lessons: Modern Design Theory* (2004). Retrieved 25 October 2022, from www.typotheque.com/articles/ writing_lessons_modern_design_theory

8.2 Typography as a Language

Michael Twyman has observed that 'Typography can legitimately be seen as visual linguistics and should be studied in relation to the wider use of language'.[162] It should be noted that by 'visual linguistics', Twyman is referring to linguistics *made visible*, rather than a metaphorical 'linguistics of the visual' or the 'language of vision' examined by Lupton. Language has been defined as a system in which component parts are organised in different ways to different effect. In this sense the properties of typographic space align very well to those of its linguistic counterpart, and the attributes that would define it as a language have been addressed in turn in the previous chapters. We have seen that the organisation of typographic space is systematic, using codified systems of interval and measurement at several levels. It has its own graphic form in the counterforms and interior spaces of letters, integral to the act of writing and the printing of the written word. This would include both the lexicon of spaces that convey specific meanings (indents, line-spaces) and the compound spaces that convey wider associative values (margins, leading, asymmetric white space and the column margins within a grid). As we will see, it reflects the concepts of morphology in the spaces between letters, and of syntax in the spatial relationships between words, lines, and margins.

A Lexicon of Space

Typographic space has a specialist lexicon of technical terms, but viewing it as a language requires the further idea of a 'visual lexicon'. One of the linguistic definitions of a lexicon is 'the complete set of meaningful units in a language'. In this context these would necessarily be units of space, including indents, leading, and other spatial variations examined in previous chapters. As we have seen, these are codified in relation to the em-square and, as Burnhill and others have shown, have a specific set of meanings formed in relation to the

---

[162] M. Twyman, *The Graphic Presentation of Language* (Amsterdam: John Benjamins, 1982)

linguistic units that surround them. Nordquist summarises language as comprising the following components:[163]

Semantics

Linguistic semantics has been defined as the study of how languages organise and express meanings, and the organisation of meanings is one of the most important attributes of typographic space. The web designer Mark Boulton makes the lucid point that documents have a conceptual structure, and graphic structures can be made that reflect those conceptual structures.[164]

Phonology

Typographic space has a phonological value in denoting the intervals or silences required by oral communication, considered in Chapter 7 in relation to the typesetting of poetry. The counterforms of inter-word-spaces might be described as a 'counter-phonology' – an organised pattern of silences. The breaking of word-units into letter units for emphasis discussed in Chapter 3 marks a deliberate interruption to voicing of successive word-shapes. Multiples of space units on either the horizontal or vertical axes are read not only as semantic signals but as multiplied intervals of silence.

Syntax

Nordquist defines syntax as 'the rules that govern the way that words combine to form phrases, clauses and sentences'. An equivalent 'visual syntax' governs relationships between the different orders of typographic space addressed in the chapters of this book; the relationship between letter-space and word-space, word-space and interlinear space, interlinear space and margin space, and the significance of typographic conventions such as the indent. It is through the use of this syntax that typographic space

---

[163] R, Nordquist (2020). Retrieved 25 October 2022, from www.thoughtco.com/syntax-grammar-1692182

[164] M. Boulton, *Semantic Typography: Bridging the XHTML Gap* (2005). Retrieved 24 October 2022, from https://markboulton.co.uk/journal/semantic-typography-bridging-the-xhtml-gap/

provides commentary and contextualisation of the text and therefore functions as a metalanguage.

8.3 Metalanguage

While typographic space meets many of the criteria to be considered as a language in its own right, its capacity to communicate independent of written content is less significant than its scope for interaction with written languages. It 'reflects upon' the text, adding tone and nuance, and so interacts with it both descriptively and analytically. For this reason it can be considered a *metalanguage*: a form of language or set of terms used for the description or analysis of another language. In applying the language of typographic space we are using a visual language to describe a verbal one, applying what El Lissitzky described as 'a reading of optics not phonetics'.[165] Concepts of 'visual language' in design tend to focus upon expressive qualities, but the examples considered in previous chapters confirm that typographic space is not merely expressive of particular values, but articulate: susceptible to complex readings through the controlled relationship of its parts. These enable typographic space to 'talk about' the linguistic content that it supports and contains. The 'object language' or language under study is written language, and the metalanguage used talk about it is typographic space. Considering typographic space as a metalanguage allows us to apply the term 'language' to a set of material properties, as a means towards offering a metalinguistic analysis of verbal content. Applying a visual metalanguage to a verbal language parallels exactly the relationships we have considered between the visual design of the page and the textual content of the book.

We are used to considering typographic space simply as a backdrop; the correlative without which language would be invisible. Beatrice Warde's analogy of typography as a 'crystal goblet',[166] as well as elevating the

---

[165] L. Lissitzky, 'Topography of Typography'. In M. Bierut, J. Helfand, S. Heller, R. Poynor (eds.), *Looking Closer 3* (New York: Allworth, 1999), p. 23

[166] B. Warde, 'The Crystal Goblet or Printing Should Be Invisible'. In M. Bierut, J. Helfand, S. Heller, R. Poynor (eds.) *Looking Closer 3* (New York: Allworth, 1999), p. 21

virtues of a stylistically 'invisible' typography, assumes also that typographic space could be invisible or transparent, a modernist ideal that has by now proved unattainable. Typographic space conforms to the linguistic definition of a 'natural language' in that it has developed organically rather than being artificially constructed. As we have seen, successive systems of production have left their mark upon its development, but its evolution has been a gradual sequence of responses to the requirements of written language, and the constraints and affordances of successive technologies. Metalinguistic awareness is an acquired skill, and this applies equally to 'reading' the metalanguage of typographic space. Like language use, however, skills can be absorbed tacitly through examples, rather than requiring specific instruction, definition or conscious understanding. Just as the skills of writing grammatically may be absorbed simply through wider reading of well-written texts, without any knowledge of the terminology and 'rules' of grammar, the metalinguistic implications signalled by leading, justification, or asymmetric margins can interpreted by a reader unaware that such terms exist.

David Crystal's 1997 keynote paper *Toward a Typographical Linguistics*[167] identified a knowledge gap in research and study at the intersection of the two disciplines. Crystal says: 'It seems to me that the explication of printed language needs the expertise of both typographers and linguists, in order to provide a complete description of its forms and structures and a satisfactory explanation of its functions and effects.' He identifies the need 'for linguists to become more interested in 'the properties of graphic substance' and 'for typographers to become more interested in the linguistic properties of printed language'. These themes are developed by Jefferson Maia in his 2018 thesis *Towards a Typographical Linguistics: The Semantics-Pragmatics of Typographic Emphasis in Discourse.*[168] He references Crystal's point that 'the fundamental question for a typographical

[167] D. Crystal, 'Toward a Typographical Linguistics', p. 7

[168] Maia J. *Toward a Typographical Linguistics: The Semantics-Pragmatics of Typographic Emphasis in Discourse* (2018). Retrieved 25 October 2022, from https://scholarcommons.sc.edu/etd/4922/

linguist must be how the various features of typography convey meaning or hinder its expression',[169] but the devices he identifies for emphasis and signalling make only limited reference to the spatial properties of type. This reflects a widespread assumption that these meaningful features are limited to graphic devices and variations in the form of letters, rather than the organisation of the space around them.

8.4 The Frame

Discussions of metalanguage frequently use the analogy of the picture frame. The manner in which a visual image is 'framed', and the environment in which it is presented, signal cultural value and direct the expectations of the audience. This phenomenon emerged as a preoccupation of the twentieth-century avant-garde, in key examples such as Marcel Duchamp's *Fountain*. Encountering a urinal in the hallowed space of the gallery or museum invites interpretation and enquiry of a kind one would never associate with the object in its more familiar context. This recontextualisation is also a key dynamic in the work of artists like Andy Warhol, in which scale and gallery space force a reappraisal of purposely banal imagery. The picture frame, or the environmental 'frame' of a gallery space, invokes a metalanguage closely equivalent to that of space on the printed page. The margins which confine a text-block are of course a 'frame', and the visual qualities of this frame serve to prompt, direct, or, indeed, interpret the content they surround. As discussed in Chapters 4 and 5, the amount of space in leading and margins indicates the capacity for interlinear readings and marginalia; the 'closed' or 'open' nature of the text. They signal the level of care and attention the author anticipates from the reader and indicate the conditions in which the page is to be read. The framing of a text within a designed arrangement of typographic space may be governed by the aesthetics of added value or the imperatives of page economy, may evoke tradition through symmetry or modernity through asymmetry, to establish the preconditions of the reading experience.

[169] ibid.

8.5 Conclusion: Space as Syntax

As we have established over the successive chapters of this book, typography is concerned with 'outside and inside' at multiple levels, and the connection Bachelard makes between these concepts and the 'spatiality of thought' supports the hypothesis that typographic space, rather than being a passive or transparent surface on which thought is enacted, is an articulate (and active) medium for the connection and organisation of ideas. Linguistics provides us with the means to discuss the codified language of typographic space, and thus make explicit an implicit metalanguage. Nordquist's definition of syntax, referring to the way that elements combine to form larger units, applies equally to the spatial structure of the page, in which the relationships of letter space, word-space, leading, and margins form a single unit in the composition of the page: a unit composed of the common material of typographic space. It is through the use of this syntax that typographic space functions as a metalanguage, and articulates both a commentary on and contextualisation of the text. Space guides and directs the reading process and establishes the relationships between different orders of information. It also provides us with signals as to how we should read; framing the expectations with which we are to approach the text.

Previous chapters have shown the ways in which this metalanguage is enabled and defined by the technics of printing and the subsequent development of typography. Smeijers makes the important distinction that 'in typography the composition of the word, as well as the making of the letters, is regulated by machine fabrication',[170] while the concept and practice of leading exemplifies the period in which Kinross describes typography becoming aware of itself.[171] We can conclude that the standardisation of character space and word-space distinguishes type from lettering or writing, while the manipulation of space between lines of type differentiates typography from printing. The geometry and profile of the resulting negative space differentiates typographic idioms and identifies the philosophies that they represent, notably distinguishing modernism from 'classical' tradition. These features combine in the larger unit of the page to provide an articulate metalanguage of typographic space that informs and enhances the content it contains.

[170] Smeijers, *Counterpunch*, p. 22 [171] Kinross, *Modern Typography*, p. 9

Bibliography

Bachelard, G. (1994). *The Poetics of Space*. Translated by Jolas, M. Boston: Beacon Press.

Banks, C. (2003). Edward Johnston and Letter Spacing. In Berry, J., Randle, J. (eds.), *Type and Typography*. New York: Mark Batty, pp. 347–353.

Beier, S. (2012). *Reading Letters: Designing for Legibility*. Amsterdam: Bis.

Bierut, M. (2003). *Graphic Design and the New Certainties*. Retrieved 25 October 2022, from https://designobserver.com/feature/graphic-design-and-the-new-certainties/1617.

Blokland, F. (2016). *On the Origin of Patterning in Movable Latin Type*. Retrieved 25 October 2022, from https://hdl.handle.net/1887/43556.

Boag, A. (1996). Typographic Measurement: A Chronology. In *Typography Papers*, 1, Reading: Department of Typography and Graphic Communication, University of Reading.

Bollnow, O. F. (2011). *Human Space*. Translated by Shuttleworth, C. London: Hyphen.

Boulton, M. (2005). *Semantic Typography: Bridging the XHTML Gap*. Retrieved 24 October 2022, from https://markboulton.co.uk/journal/semantic-typography-bridging-the-xhtml-gap/.

Bringhurst, R. (1997). *The Elements of Typographic Style*. Vancouver: Hartley and Marks.

Burnhill, P. (2003). *Type Spaces: In-house Norms in the Typography of Aldus Manutius*. London: Hyphen.

Carter, R., Day, B., Meggs, P. (2006). *Typographic Design: Form and Communication*. Hoboken: Wiley.

Cinamon, G. (2000). *Rudolf Koch: Letterer, Type Designer, Teacher*. Delaware: Oak Knoll.

Cobbing, B. (1989). *Square Poem*. Retrieved 24 December 2022, from https://gammm.org/2022/06/18/square-poem-bob-cobbing–1989/.

Crystal D. (1998). 'Toward a Typographical Linguistics'. *Type*, 2. 1, pp. 7–23.

Dair, C. (1995). *Design with Type*. Toronto: University of Toronto Press.

Dowding, G. (1954). *Finer Points in the Spacing and Arrangement of Type*. London: Wace.

Drucker, J. (2006). Quantum Leap: Beyond Literal Materiality. In Bierut, M., Drenttel, W., Heller, S. (eds.), *Looking Closer 5*. New York: Allworth, pp. 26–32.

Drucker, J. (1984). *Letterpress Language: Typography as a Medium for the Visual Representation of Language*. Cambridge: MIT.

de Campos, A., Pignatari, D., de Campos, H. (1958). *Pilot Plan for Concrete Poetry*. Retrieved 25 October 2022, from https://ubu-mirror.ch/papers/noigandres01.html.

Fletcher, A. (2003). *The Art of Looking Sideways*. London: Phaidon.

Gayford, M., Sylvester, D. (1998). *Patrick Heron*. London: Tate.

Gill, E. (2013). *An Essay on Typography*. London: Penguin.

Hendel, R. (1998). *On Book Design*. Yale: Yale University Press.

Highsmith, C. (2020). *Inside Paragraphs: Typographic Fundamentals*. New York: Princeton Architectural Press.

Hochuli, J. (2015). *Detail in Typography*. Montreuil: Éditions B42.

Hoffman, A. (1988). *A Graphic Design Manual*. London: Academy Editions.

Hollis, R. (2006). *Swiss Graphic Design*. London: Laurence King.

Hunt, R. (2020). *Advanced Typography*. London: Bloomsbury.

Hutt, A. (1972). *Fournier: The Compleat Typographer*. London: Frederick Muller.

de Jong, C. W. (2008). *Jan Tschichold: Master Typographer*. London: Thames and Hudson.

Kindersley, D. (2001). LOGOS: Letterspacing with a Computer. In Jury, D. (ed.), *Typographic Writing*. Stroud: ISTD, pp. 174–178.

Kinross, R. (1994). *Modern Typography*. London: Hyphen.

Kinross, R. (2000). *Anthony Froshaug Typography and Texts*. London: Hyphen.

Kinross, R. (2002). *Unjustified Texts*. London: Hyphen.

Krauss, R. (1999). *A Voyage on the North Sea: Art in the Age of the Postmodern Condition*. London: Thames and Hudson.

Larson, K. (2022). *The Science of Word Recognition*. Retrieved 25 October 2022, from https://docs.microsoft.com/en-us/typography/develop/word-recognition.

Li Er Lao Tzu. (1997). *Tao Te Ching*. Translated by Waley, A. and Wilkinson, R. Ware: Wordsworth.

Lissitzky, L. (1999). Topography of Typography. In Beirut, M., Helfand, J., Heller, J. Poynor, R. (eds.), *Looking Closer 3*. New York: Allworth.

Lommen, M. (2012). *The Book of Books*. London: Thames and Hudson.

Lupton, E. (2004). *Writing Lessons: Modern Design Theory*. Retrieved 25 October 2022, from www.typotheque.com/articles/writing_lessons_modern_design_theory.

Lupton, E. (2004). *Deconstruction and Graphic Design: History Meets Theory*. Retrieved 26 October 2022, from www.typotheque.com/articles/deconstruction_and_graphic_design_history_meets_theory.

Lupton, E. (2000). Visual Syntax. In Swanson, G. (ed.), *Graphic Design and Reading*. New York: Allworth.

Lupton, E. and Miller, J. A. (1994). A Natural History of Typography. In Bierut, M., Drenttel, W., Heller, S. and Holland, D. K. (eds.), *Looking Closer: Critical Writings on Graphic Design*. New York: Allworth.

Maia, J. (2018). *Toward a Typographical Linguistics: The Semantics-Pragmatics of Typographic Emphasis in Discourse*. Retrieved 25 October 2022, from https://scholarcommons.sc.edu/etd/4922/.

Maier, S. (2015). *Design Dissection*. Retrieved 25 October 2022, from http://thesis2015.micadesign.org/sally/.

Martin, D. (1989). *An Outline of Book Design*. London: Blueprint.

McGann, J. (1993). *Black Riders*. Princeton: Princeton University Press.

Meynell, F. and Simon, H. (1973). *Fleuron Anthology*. London: Ernest Benn.

Moholy-Nagy, L. (1999). The New Typography. In Beirut, M., Helfand, J., Heller, J., Poynor, R. (eds.), *Looking Closer 3*. New York: Allworth, pp. 21–22.

Morison, S. (1996). *First Principles of Typography*. Leiden: Academic Press Leiden.

Muller-Brockmann, J. (1981). *Grid Systems in Graphic Design*. Sulgen: Niggli.

Nash, P. (2016). Scaleboard: The Material of Interlinear Spacing before 'Leading'. *Journal of the Printing Historical Society*. 25, pp. 71–83.

Nash, R., Williams, R. (1999) *Revival of Calligraphy (19th and 20th Centuries)*. Retrieved 25 October 2022, from www.britannica.com/art/calligraphy/Revival-of-calligraphy-19th-and-20th-centuries.

Nin, A. (1971). *The Diary of Anaïs Nin 1939–1944*. Vol. 3. Boston: Mariner.

Noordzij, G. (2005). *The Stroke: Theory of Writing*. Translated by Enneson, P. London: Hyphen.

Nordquist, R. (2020). Retrieved 25 October 2022, from www.thoughtco.com/syntax-grammar.

Papazian, H. (2000). Improving the Tool. In Swanson, G. (ed.), *Graphic Design and Reading*. New York: Allworth.

Phillips, T. (2005). *A Humument*. 4th ed. London: Thames and Hudson.

Ritscher, P. (2014). *Hand Setting*. Retrieved October 25, 2022, from www.briarpress.org/37356.

Ronell, A. and Eckersley, R. (1991). *The Telephone Book : Technology, Schizophrenia, Electric speech*. Lincoln: University of Nebraska Press.

Rosner, C. (1953). *Type: Principles and Application*. Wisbech: Balding and Mansell.

Saenger, P. (2000). *Space between Words: The Origins of Silent Reading*. Redwood City: Stanford University Press.

Schwitters, K. (1932). *Ursonate*. Retrieved 24 December 2022, from https://web.archive.org/web/20060216143920/http://ubu.clc.wvu.edu/historical/schwitters/ursonate.html.

Shaw, P. (2006). W. A. Dwiggins: Jack of all Trades, Master of More Than One. *Linotype Matrix*. 4.2, pp. 37–47.

Simon, O. (1954). Introduction to Typography. London: Pelican.

Simpson, N. (ed.). (2012) *Notes from the Cosmic Typewriter*. London: Occasional papers.

Smeijers, F. (2011). *Counterpunch*. London: Hyphen.

Spencer, H. (1968). *The Visible Word*. London: Royal College of Art.

Symons, A. J. A. (1973). An Unacknowledged Movement in Fine Printing. In Meynell, F., Simon, H. (eds.), *Fleuron Anthology*. London: Ernest Benn, pp. 301–325.

Thomas, K. (2015). Rudolf von Larisch: Investigating and Analysing the Ideas and Theories of a Lettering Reformer, unpublished Master's thesis, Monash University.

Tracy, W. (1986). *Letters of Credit*. Boston: Godine.

Tschichold, J. (1991). *The Form of the Book*. London: Lund Humphries.

Tschichold, J. (1998). *The New Typography*. Translated by McLean, R. London: University of California Press.

Tullett, B. (2014). *Typewriter Art: A Modern Anthology*. London: Laurence King.

Twyman, M. (1982). *The Graphic Presentation of Language*. Amsterdam: John Benjamins.

Walker, S. (2001). *Typography and Language in Everyday Life*. Harlow: Pearson.

Warde, B. (1999). The Crystal Goblet or Printing Should be Invisible. In Bierut, M., Helfand, J., Heller, J., Poynor, R. (eds.), *Looking Closer 3*. New York: Allworth, pp. 56–59.

Weingart, W. (1973). *Elements in a New Context*. Retrieved 25 October 2022.

Winterson, J. (2003) *The Hole of Life*. Retrieved 25 October 2022, from www.tate.org.uk/art/artists/dame-barbara-hepworth-1274/hole-life.

Cambridge Elements ☰

Publishing and Book Culture

SERIES EDITOR

Samantha Rayner

University College London

Samantha Rayner is Professor of Publishing and Book Cultures at UCL. She is also Director of UCL's Centre for Publishing, co-Director of the Bloomsbury CHAPTER (Communication History, Authorship, Publishing, Textual Editing and Reading) and co-Chair of the Bookselling Research Network.

ASSOCIATE EDITOR

Leah Tether

University of Bristol

Leah Tether is Professor of Medieval Literature and Publishing at the University of Bristol. With an academic background in medieval French and English literature and a professional background in trade publishing, Leah has combined her expertise and developed an international research profile in book and publishing history from manuscript to digital.

ABOUT THE SERIES

This series aims to fill the demand for easily accessible, quality texts
available for teaching and research in the diverse and dynamic fields
of Publishing and Book Culture. Rigorously researched and
peer-reviewed Elements will be published under themes, or
'Gatherings'. These Elements should be the first check point for
researchers or students working on that area of publishing and book
trade history and practice: we hope that, situated so logically at
Cambridge University Press, where academic publishing in the UK
began, it will develop to create an unrivalled space where these
histories and practices can be investigated and preserved.

Cambridge Elements ☰

Publishing and Book Culture

Typography and the Book

Gathering Editor: Will Hill

Will Hill is Emeritus Associate Professor of Graphic Design at
Cambridge School of Art, Anglia Ruskin University. As
a designer, teacher and writer his research, teaching and
professional practice are based around typography, text-image
relationships and the visual form of language.

ELEMENTS IN THE GATHERING

A full series listing is available at: www.cambridge.org/EPBC

Printed in the United States
by Baker & Taylor Publisher Services